W9-AZW-528

Sexual Hauntings
Through the Ages

Sexual Hauntings Through the Ages

Colin Waters

Dorset Press
New York

Originally published as *Familiar Spirits: Sexual Hauntings through the Ages.*

Copyright © 1993 by Colin Waters
All rights reserved.

This edition published by Dorset Press,
a division of Barnes & Noble, Inc.,
by arrangement with Robert Hale Ltd.

1994 Dorset Press

ISBN 1-56619-621-3

Printed and bound in the United States of America

M 9 8 7 6 5 4 3 2

Contents

6   · CONTENTS ·

Introduction

Whether one personally believes in ghosts or not, it cannot be denied that ghost stories are fascinating to read and discuss. Many would admit that their own beliefs on the subject lie midway between the extremes of the firm believer and the confirmed sceptic, and each has his or her own theories concerning these strange hauntings and their causes. There are those who have never seen a ghost yet are firmly convinced of their presence, whilst others claim to have seen ghosts, yet illogically remain disbelievers whilst readily admitting the dichotomy.

Theories abound as to what ghosts are and why they manifest themselves in such a variety of ways. As is usually the case, theories always lead to more questions. Are all such experiences due to the same cause or are there a variety of different types of spectres, ghosts, apparitions, spirits, entities and the like? Is it possible to see ghosts of living people, or of oneself (the *doppelgänger*)? Why are some silent, whilst others scream, cry, or carry out conversations with the living? And why are some 'solid' whilst others are transparent, whispy or even invisible?

Though many have sought to answer such questions, science has yet to find a positive and definitive solution to any of them. Some patterns have emerged over the years, such as the type of ghost whose haunting repeats time and time again without change (almost like some strange ancient video picture which somehow uses the atmosphere as its screen). Such hauntings often appear to occur on the anniversary of an event such as a murder, hanging or other emotionally-charged incident. Others occur spontaneously, though again, strong emotions or an atmosphere imagined (or created) by the 'viewer' would seem to influence the appearance of ghosts and the emanation of strange poltergeist activity.

Emotion I believe, is one of the major keys to the mind-altering state which allows one to experience the presence or sighting of ghosts. The stronger the emotion, the higher the chance of 'the misty veil' between this world and another (whatever the *other world* is) being lifted.

Sexual emotion must rank (along with fear and love) as one of the three strongest mental energy states known to mankind. It is little wonder then that a wide variety of hauntings are either sexual in nature (i.e., the ghost acts in a sexual manner), or are a manifestation of overt or suppressed sexual feelings.

This book is an attempt to catalogue a variety of different ghostly activities, all with a sexual theme. I have endeavoured to ensure that only factual cases have been included, and have recorded the facts as found. Where variations of a particular story have been found during research, I have endeavoured to either give the reader an account of these, or have followed the most often recorded version of the events. In only a few (more modern) stories did I have cause to doubt their authenticity (at least in part), and where doubt may exist, this has been made clear to the reader in the text. In truth, many (perhaps most) of the cases would be difficult to verify satisfactorily, mainly because writers in the past have changed names (and in some cases locations) in order to protect their informants. Those which I personally felt had been put forward as fact, but were in all probability fiction, have been excluded from this compilation.

I hope that the reader will enjoy the stories that follow, and draw his or her own conclusions as to what in reality causes and constitutes a 'haunting'. My only request is that readers who are sceptical of such stories do not close their minds completely to the fact that ghosts *may* exist, whilst those who believe without question all stories of ghostly events should perhaps temper their unswerving beliefs with a touch of scepticism. In this way, all may meet on common ground, and in doing so may further the cause of genuine investigation into paranormal events.

As Thomas Carlyle (1795–1881) advised us whilst considering the reality of ghosts:

> Sweep away the illusion of time; compress our threescore years into three minutes ... Are we not spirits, that are shaped into a body, into an Appearance; and that fade away into air and invisibility? This is no metaphor, it is a simple fact: we start out of Nothingness, take figure and are apparitions ... Ghosts! there are a thousand million walking the earth ... some half hundred have vanished from it, some half hundred have arisen in it, ere thy watch ticks once ... we not only carry each a future ghost within him; but are, in very deed, Ghosts!

Colin Waters, Whitby 1992

1   Naked Embrace
at Rattlesden Rectory

Old Rattlesden Rectory (Suffolk) was well known for its ghosts. In 1908 a local landlord was fond of telling itinerant travellers of his own experience in the building which had been built upon an ancient mound, believed by many to have once been topped by an ancient mystical stone circle.

As a young man the landlord had been a carpenter and had been called upon to visit the old rectory to repair a number of rotten floorboards and panels. However, because the weather was so bad that day, he had held off making the journey until it had begun to get dark.

Once within the rectory the carpenter began repair work in the old pantry, where some panels had begun to rot and decay. As he worked he was conscious that before setting off, he had been warned to be careful of the rats which were said to have infested the building, and apparently ran freely around the many narrow passageways and tiny chambers that formed a veritable rabbit warren of nooks and crannies.

The poor light together with the decayed state of the place obviously made him uneasy as he worked alone, repairing the panelling, and before long he became very aware of a stale musty smell which at first he put down to the dampness and the presence of rats. It was not long however before he began to feel extremely uneasy, almost as if he was being watched as he worked. The atmosphere of the place began to feel heavy and hostile and without realizing it, his pulse began to race as he consciously speeded up his work in an effort to get finished.

As he worked, his eyes were continuously drawn to the half-open pantry door, upon which he had thrown a dust-sheet, and where he half expected to see someone or even worse, something (rats?), peeping at him through the darkening gap.

Aware that his imagination might now be playing tricks on him, he at first ignored a slight rustling sound coming from the direction of the door. Was it really his imagination? He stopped and listened hard. Yes, there *was* a definite rustling sound. The noise seemed to be getting gradually louder. It grew in intensity until before long he heard a light whistling or wheezing together with a sound of rattling tins or pans, followed by the sight of two eerie hands which suddenly appeared over the top of the door, grabbing the dust-sheet and pulling it into the darkness of the room behind.

Though it did cross his mind that this might be some

prank to scare the living daylights out of him, the young carpenter remained almost rigid, resisting any urge to face the prankster behind the door for fear of finding some unearthly spirit or monster ready to squeeze the living daylights out of him with its eerie ghostly hands.

The rustling and rattling sounds began again, followed by a low uncanny whistling sound and then the door bursting open to reveal the dust-sheet gliding slowly through the air towards him in a jerking motion, first stopping, then moving nearer. His eyes widened as he perceived in the dim light a human head rocking on top of the sheet, almost as if severed, and attached to the cloth with a pin or string. The head seemed almost deflated like some rotten apple or a punctured pig's bladder, and though no eyes or nose were visible, a long limp blue tongue hung from its hideous mouth.

Though by now he was terrified by what he still half-believed was a joke, the adrenalin rushing through his body spurred him to action. He quickly picked up one of the large hammers he had been working with and stood, arm raised ready, to rain blows upon whoever or whatever it was that now threatened him. 'Stop buggering about and come out of that sheet,' he yelled in defiance, but to no avail. The eerie rocking head now began to move towards him at a faster pace – only diverting its course slightly to push past him to the corner of the small space in which he had been working – and finally dropped the sheet to the floor.

Far from finding a grinning prankster behind it, as he now expected, the carpenter found he was facing a horrifying ghostly naked figure, with wizened skin which was drawn tightly together like some long dead corpse. Its blotchy brown body with indistinct facial features now began to crouch low in the corner giving off the terrible smell which the young man had noticed whilst he was working on the panelling shortly before.

Throughout all this the young carpenter began to feel a distinct atmosphere of evil, almost as if the ghostly figure was trying to infiltrate his consciousness and get its spirit inside his shaking body. Though the space was small the unearthly figure began to feel its way once more towards him, almost as if completely blind, and as the stench became stronger and stronger the man realized that it and he were on a collision course which he could not avoid. Before long he was being groped by its evil hands, finally ending in a sickly embrace. It now had its cold cheeks pressed against his own, seemingly in an effort to have its unearthly lips meet with his in a sickening kiss.

This was the last thing the man remembered of the incident, for the terror had been so much that he had fainted on the spot. When he came round it was darker than ever, but the evil atmosphere had left the room. Grabbing his things together he rushed from the building, vowing never to set foot in it again.

What was this strange apparition? Could it have been an elaborate hoax? Apparently not, for an avid ghost hunter Robert Thurston Hopkins decided to follow up the story in 1941, thirty-three years after hearing the story at first hand from the landlord.

Though disappointed to find that the original haunted building had been pulled down in 1892, the intrepid ghost hunter was well received in a new building on the site, occupied by a vicar who was able to produce pictures taken by the last resident of the building. This previous tenant was a Reverend Olorenshaw, who had described it as a 'rat infested collection of rooms and corridors entirely given over to the powers of darkness'. With the photographs were notes indicating accounts of hauntings and happenings experienced over the years. One of these entries contained a description of the 'haunted pantry' which evidently had had a coffin-shaped tiled pattern in the centre of the floor.

On demolition of the building, the pantry floor tiles were uprooted to reveal the remains of an actual coffin and a decaying skeleton. Following enquiries the skeleton was positively identified as that of Robert Bumstead who died in great debt in 1780. To prevent seizure of the body by creditors, Bumstead's body had been hidden beneath the floor of the pantry and had remained there until found during the demolition of the building.

Though reburied within the nearby churchyard, the ghost described by the old landlord continued to haunt the area until an exorcism was ordered by a local priest. This laying of the ghost ceremony was performed apparently successfully as no further hauntings were recorded and it would seem Robert Bumstead finally rested his spirit in peace at last.

2 Pattie's Back Yard

It was 1969 when Pattie Morgan moved into a poky little flat in rather a run-down area of Wellington, New Zealand. Aged twenty, she had recently obtained a job as an air hostess with one of the major airlines, and her new increased income had encouraged her to find her own place to live. The flat was only about two miles from her parents' house, but more to the point (as far as she was concerned), her boyfriend Greg Parker lived only two blocks away. It was he who had encouraged her to apply for a job with the airline company where he worked as a steward.

Though run-down, the building was clean, with its own back yard where there was a kind of outhouse. The shed had only three walls and a roof and was used to house the dustbin and little else. Pattie decided that she would turn the yard into a garden, and eventually convert the outhouse into a proper garden shed. One of the first jobs, she told herself, was to put a gate on the yard to keep out all the neighbourhood dogs which were obviously raiding the dustbin and making a mess in the yard.

Pattie's first week in the new flat was spent rearranging the old furniture. At her boyfriend's suggestion, and with his help, she altered the layout of the accommodation so that the bedroom furniture which was upstairs was taken downstairs to the ground floor level, and the sitting-room furniture (previously on the ground floor), was taken upstairs, giving her a view over the stark yard wall to the street below. From her window she could at least now see the passers-by who consisted mainly of old people from the flats around.

It was one July evening about a week after moving in that Pattie looked out from her upstairs window. In the yard, which was mostly well lit by a street light, she noticed something moving in the shadows of the outhouse. She heard the dustbin lid rattle and thinking one of the local dogs was raiding the dustbin, opened the window and shouted. To her surprise it was an old man who responded to her call and shuffled quickly away. He seemed to hitch up his trousers as he made for the open gateway, and quickly vanished into the night.

'Poor old bugger,' Pattie said to herself, feeling sorry for the old man, who she assumed was a tramp who had been gathering what morsels of food he could from the bin. Over the next few weeks the tramp returned on a number of occasions, and although Pattie didn't exactly relish the idea of the old man going through the contents of her dustbin, she could not bring herself to say anything to him, telling herself that Greg would be fixing the gap into the yard with a gate soon anyway.

Time passed and the tramp became a regular visitor. Though he thought he was unseen, Pattie would watch him through a gap in the curtains as he rummaged through the bin. Sometimes he would sit for a while, resting his back against the wall in the dark, and looked as if he was emptying his pockets and doing something with their contents. Pattie's patience began to wear rather thin.

The crunch came when one morning Pattie awoke and looked out of the window. She immediately got onto the phone to her boyfriend.

'Greg, I've had enough of this,' she said angrily. 'The old bugger's taken to sleeping in the yard now, he's still there, and what's more he's playing with himself!'

Greg laughed. 'Playing with himself? You mean…?'

Pattie spelt it out in no uncertain terms. The old man was masturbating in the yard and she wanted Greg down here 'NOW' to move him.

Greg's reaction was one of amused indifference, but he went round immediately to ask the man to move. Arriving at the flat, he went immediately to the yard but found no one there. To put Pattie's mind at east, he immediately went round to the nearest hardware store and purchased the materials to make a six foot high door to block off the yard and prevent the tramp's return.

'That'll do the job,' said Greg, as he finished the door. 'Six foot high, and padlocked from the inside.'

Pattie was relieved, and took the padlock key from him. Now she could get her yard tidied up and begin buying plants for her garden.

She awoke two days later, deciding that she would go down to the garden centre to buy some grass seed, but as she pulled back the curtains of her downstairs bedroom, she recoiled in horror. There opposite her, sitting in the outhouse, was the dirty old figure of the tramp. Again he was playing with himself, but this time he was obviously aware of Pattie, and sat staring at her with a silly grin on his face. Pattie immediately reclosed the curtains and phoned her boyfriend, saying that somehow the old man had opened the new door and was 'at it again', in her outhouse.

Greg was now angry and concerned. Rushing round to the back of the flat, he tried the door. It was still locked. Fearing that Pattie might be in some danger, he raced to the front of the building to find Pattie waiting at the open door. Greg indicated that they had got the old man trapped, as even if he had climbed over the six foot wall, there was no way he could get out again. Going inside, Greg picked up the phone ready to call the police, asking Pattie at the same time to peek through the curtains to see what the man was doing now. To her surprise the man had once more vanished, and Greg put down the telephone in disgust. Examining the yard, both Pattie and Greg were at a loss as to how the old man could have got out. The wall was too tall to climb, even for Greg, and there was no other way out besides through the house door (which had been locked).

'Maybe he's a ghost,' Greg said jokingly.

That day Greg helped Pattie lay a lawn, and brought his camera, so that should the tramp return, he could photograph him as evidence to give to the police. He decided he would stay the night.

Next morning Pattie carefully opened a chink in the curtains.

'He's there again,' she whispered, 'and the dirty bugger's at it again.'

Greg rushed for his camera, and darted upstairs to photograph the old man from the top window. Looking out he could see nothing. 'He's got away again,' he shouted.

'No he hasn't, he's still there,' Pattie immediately shouted back.

Puzzled, Greg rushed downstairs to the ground floor only to find that Pattie now agreed she couldn't see him either. The couple decided that even though they hadn't captured the old tramp, they would now be able to find his escape route, as he had been sitting in the outhouse and must have crossed the newly laid lawn to arrive and escape, leaving clear footprints in the freshly raked soil.

No footprints were to be found, and Greg began to wonder if Pattie was making up the story. After all, he had never seen the old man, and how could anybody enter and leave a locked yard with a six foot wall, not to mention avoiding making footprints in newly raked soil? Pattie insisted that what she had seen was not a figment of her imagination and asked Greg to stay with her all day, and another night. Greg reluctantly agreed.

During the day, the pair visited the garden centre round the corner to buy more plants for the yard. Browsing through the stocks of gardening books they struck up a conversation with the owner, who asked if they were new to the district. Pattie said she was and asked if the shop owner had seen anything of a tramp in the district lately. The owner said he hadn't and Pattie let the matter drop. Conversation turned again to Pattie's new home when the shop owner asked where she lived. On giving her address he laughed to himself, annoying her boyfriend who asked what he thought was so funny.

'Oh,' said the garden centre owner, 'I was just thinking … It's a good job you didn't live there six months ago … the previous lady Pattie Lindsey, was troubled by the old man who lived next door … He used to always be in her dustbin, looking for anything he could scrounge ... and making sexy suggestions to her too.' Seeing the look of unease on Pattie's face, the shopkeeper attempted to ease her concern. 'But don't worry love,' he said, 'the dirty old sod died ... had a heart attack he did ... playing with himself in Pattie's back yard.'

3 The Brothel for Ghosts and Spectres

Up to a hundred years ago, there was a well-known house in West Bow, Edinburgh, where people would gather to watch through the windows of a derelict house to see the sexual debauchery said to be practised by ghosts, almost every night. The house came to be known as the 'ghosts' whorehouse' and though the exact site of the building is now lost to memory, it is still said that a ghostly tapping stick can be heard in the Grassmarket, and that a burned and blackened face of one of the revellers named 'Grizel' is still occasionally to be seen.

The house in question was the home of Edinburgh's commander of the city guard in 1649, Major Thomas Weir. Weir was said to be a Jekyll and Hyde character who had the dubious honour of being in charge of the execution of the Marquis of Montrose. Though a pillar of the Presbyterian church, it is said that he never married, but instead lived (as man and wife) with his eldest sister Grizel.

This double life of the Weirs was often hinted at by those who knew the couple well, but was never brought into the open until he was tried at his own insistence in 1670, at the age of sixty-nine. At his trial, Major Weir confessed to many 'diabolical practices' including incest, making pacts with the devil and taking part in hundreds of revolting crimes, including sex with the dead.

His sister Grizel told the court that she was able to spin yarn of any quantity in the shortest of time, thanks to the couple's pacts with the devil. She also stated that Weir's power was held in his staff, which had been given to him personally by the devil.

22

Even at this early time, many were sceptical of the major's claims, and at one stage it was thought that he and his sister were insane. However, after medical examinations, the couple were pronounced of sound mind (though the sister's sanity had always been in question, for she claimed that the walking stick was often sent to do the shopping for the couple).

Neighbours who were brought in as witnesses claimed that many wicked sexual practices could be heard taking place at the couple's home, and strangely the couple confessed to practically everything which was said about them. Consequently they were both found guilty and sentenced to death by strangulation and burning.

Even the strange couple's executions were unusual. Weir was taken beyond the city walls where he was hung on a gallows at a public ceremony. His body was then burnt along with his so-called magical staff. Witnesses at the burning said that the staff twisted and turned as if it was alive, and did not go out until the major's body stopped burning. His sister Grizel was taken unconcerned to a gibbet in the Grassmarket, where to the amusement of the assembled throng, she struggled violently with the

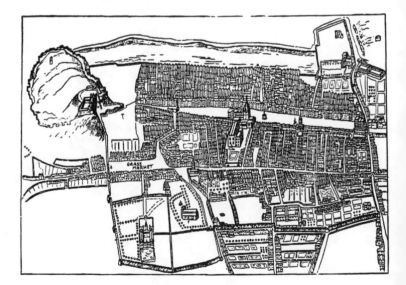

hangman, not in an attempt to save her life, but to take off her clothes. Eventually the executioner gave up the battle with Grizel, and pushed her quickly off the ladder before she had been given the normal courtesy of addressing the crowd with her last words.

From the day of the execution, it is said that no mortal would enter the house and from this time onwards it gradually fell into decay. Those who were brave (or drunk) enough would climb trees to look through the windows, or would gather at the ground floor to investigate the ghostly laughter, music and general debauchery which was said to take place. Whenever anything did happen, the house was lit by eerie lights said to look nothing like any type of lighting known at that time. Some say that these sexual antics were a sign that Weir and Grizel had returned to haunt their old home, whilst others insisted that the place had become so evil that every wicked ghost and spectre in Scotland gathered there for regular sexual orgies. The house had indeed become a brothel for ghosts and spectres, and remained so until it was demolished many years later at the request of the authorities.

4   The Bell Witch

Sexual advances by a father to a daughter, or indeed an actual sexual relationship, may have been the trigger which began a most strange series of extraordinary events known as the 'Bell Witch Hauntings'. The disturbing events which took place over a four year period in the early 1900s involved the entire household of a prosperous Tennessee farming family, but central to the story is the alleged intimate relationship of the father and daughter.

Though a number of explanations have been given for the hauntings, including fraud, ventriloquism, and the works of the devil, it was the psychoanalyst Nandor Fodor in his book *Haunted People* who put forward the controversial theory that planned or actual incest triggered off the haunting by the 'Bell Witch'. Fodor noted that many poltergeist and other hauntings were brought about by sexual and other strong emotions, and that the two main victims in the case, the daughter Betsy and the father Jack, both exhibited classic symptoms. This he concluded signified deep psychological disturbances.

Betsy would swoon and faint, indicating, Fodor explained, that the girl was leaving her normal waking state (almost as if in a trance), whilst the father began to develop a nervous tic and suffered from an inability to sleep, eat, or talk. These symptoms, Fodor believed, showed guilt and an inner suffering which had in turn triggered the ghostly manifestations.

Though the modern psychoanalyst's views may be entirely true and valid as to why the hauntings began, it is still left to others to explain the hauntings themselves, and what actually constitutes a ghost.

It was the father, John (Jack) Bell, who first came into contact with the ghostly forces, though strangely they were of animal, rather than human form.

During an inspection of one of his cornfields, Jack Bell spotted a large black dog trampling the grain. Taking aim with his gun, he succeeded in killing the animal which appeared to drop dead on the spot. However, on rushing to where it had fallen he could find no trace of the animal. (The same dog was to be seen on a number of occasions, not only by the Bell family, but by slave workers who reported it vanishing before their eyes as they attacked it with sticks.)

About a week later, Jack Bell was walking along the perimeter of the same field with his two sons, when his attention was drawn to a strange bird which had landed in an oak tree above them. The bird was larger than any turkey they had ever seen, and resembled nothing that they had ever come across before. The father and sons decided to claim the bird, and shot it from the tree. However, as the boys ran towards the area where the bird had fallen, they were amazed to find no trace of it.

On hearing the tale at the dinner table, Betsy (Jack's youngest daughter) became intrigued and decided to look for the bird herself. As she approached the field she was puzzled to see a young girl, about twelve years of age and dressed in green, swinging to and fro on a makeshift swing which was attached to the tree where her father and brothers had spotted the bird earlier. Betsy approached the girl who, like the dog and the bird, vanished into thin air before her eyes.

These seemingly harmless episodes were in fact only the start of a host of horrifying experiences. Fear began to grow as strange repeated noises began to be heard in the house – rappings at the window, growling noises coming down the chimneys, scraping noises (like fingernails on a blackboard), and clatterings as if unseen pebbles were dropping around the room. Next came the sound of birds screeching and dogs fighting *within the house* despite the fact that no creatures were anywhere to be seen. Loud bangs took place as if someone were dropping furniture on the floor above, and the sounds of breaking glass and rattling chains occurred spontaneously and fleetingly. Once, Betsy awoke to find her bedpost chipped and cracked as if some large animal had broken it with its jaws, whilst other members of the family and the servants had their hair pulled and their bodies mauled by an unseen hand. Bedclothes were pulled from them as they slept, and curtains opened and closed as they watched.

Throughout all this poltergeist activity, Betsy appeared to be the main focus. So frequent were the manifestations of the ghost within her room, that other members of the family would leave her to suffer throughout the night, blocking their ears to her screaming, and paying little heed to her tales the following morning of sexual molestation by unseen ghostly hands.

Things soon became so serious that it was decided to send Betsy away in an effort to rid both her and the house of the 'witch' forever. For a while this seemed to work, but before long Betsy was complaining of visits by the ghost to her new home. Again the hand would sexually molest her and slap her face, thighs or buttocks, leaving red marks. She began to faint frequently, or would simply 'fade away' into a state of half sleep from which she would awake feeling as though she was being choked or suffocated.

By now both the press and the psychically-minded had got wind of the hauntings, and both serious investigators and tiresome cranks congregated in the town of Adams (Tennessee). Betsy began to suffer from pins and needles in her limbs and started to vomit regularly. Some reports say that the vomit itself contained pins and needles, whilst other more sober reports emphasized the obvious stress being felt by the girl.

Seances were held in an attempt to contact the ghost, and exorcists repeatedly failed to rid the poor girl of her 'demon' until eventually one group managed to get a meaningful response using a series of knocks. On succeeding occasions the knocks became lighter, changing to a scraping, then a whistling, and eventually a whispering. The whispering sound, though at first indistinct, eventually became stronger, manifesting itself as a human voice, which mockingly repeated sermons which had been given in local churches, using foul language and sexually explicit curses. The local population were horrified by the ghost's stream of obscenities, and quickly disassociated themselves from the family, leaving other investigators to try and get to the bottom of the mystery in a series of 'question and answer sessions' with the entity.

'Who are you?' asked the investigators. The reply was as obscene as it was unhelpful.

'Where do you come from?' asked another.

'I am a spirit from everywhere,' it answered.

'Where is your main abode?' they persisted.

'I am from heaven, hell and the earth,' it answered, punctuating its faltering words with more foul language.

'Where are you now?' they questioned in an attempt to pin it down to a specific answer.

'I am in the air, in houses, everywhere, anywhere and have been for millions of years,' came the evasive reply.

Further questions followed, but the ghost refused to say more to the researchers.

The family who were by now becoming hardened to the visitations by the 'Bell Witch', began to notice that the mother (Lucy Bell) had never experienced any unpleasant effects, though she had a number of times witnessed at close hand the suffering of others in the family group. Her husband Jack had also got off relatively lightly concerning the ghost's activities, until one day when the 'witch' unexpectedly announced to the rest of the family who were gathering together, 'I am determined now to torment old Jack as long as he lives'.

The ghost was true to its words. At once, Betsy was freed from the terrible hauntings which had been plaguing her life, whilst the father began to suffer its horrifying attentions. Obscene voices followed him wherever he went around the farm, he developed a nervous tic which became progressively worse, and his tongue swelled to a terrifying degree, distorting his facial features. Periods of relative peace were interspersed with times of sheer terror and pain and his limbs began to swell, only to subside again. His sons reported seeing his shoes dragged from his feet by an unseen force, and amidst convulsions of his body, shrieks and obscene verses filled the air around him. Jack slowly recovered from the attack and with tears rolling down his cheeks, told his helpless children that he could not live much longer if these terrifying attacks were to continue.

Jack immediately took to his bed where he remained for a number of weeks, with his strength gradually dying away and his will to live seemingly evaporating. A doctor was called to attend to him and during his ministrations heard the voice of the 'Bell Witch' for himself.

'I have got him this time,' it said mockingly. It was indeed true. The twisted and tortured body of Jack Bell lasted only until the next morning, when death relieved him of his terrifying burden.

No more was heard from the ghost, and Betsy, now aged sixteen, made plans to wed a young man named Joshua Gardener. Shortly before the wedding the 'Bell Witch' carried out her final haunting as Betsy lay in her bed. As she slumbered a voice said, 'Not Gardener Betsy, please Betsy Bell don't have Josh Gardener'. The ghost, almost pleading, repeated the same phrase over and over again, night after night, until under great mental pressure, Betsy eventually gave in and cancelled her wedding plans. Following a promise to return to the house in seven years, the bizarre events ceased abruptly and Betsy lived on in peace, finally marrying Richard Powell (her former schoolmaster). Their happy marriage was short-lived however and after only about fifteen years Powell died.

The 'Bell Witch' did return as promised after the seven year period, and Lucy and her two sons experienced a number of relatively mild poltergeist-type hauntings, which gradually faded away. Betsy chose not to remarry and spent the rest of her life in peace, dying at the age of eighty-six, and taking with her to the grave any unrevealed secrets concerning her relationship with her father. She left behind one of the strangest cases of hauntings in the history of recorded ghostly activity.

5   Mary Fitton Visits Australia

Neil Cowarts, a Yorkshireman, was browsing in a second-hand bookshop one day, when he came across a small neatly-printed booklet showing the Sydney Harbour Bridge on the cover. It caught his eye because he had spent a year in Sydney during a four-year spell in Australia. The book contained a mixture of stories, poems and drawings on pages which were obviously photocopied, but still attractively presented. It was obviously the journal of some small community group or writers' circle, though the name of the publishers or printer was not given.

On the top corner of the booklet was inscribed in pencil, the price 50p, and on impulse, he decided to buy it. Though most of its contents were of little interest to Cowarts he noted a poem with background information entitled 'Mary Fitton'. The text of the page is reproduced here in its entirety:

During my stay at a flat in Mosman [an area of Sydney] I once used a ouija board with a group of friends from Redfern [another area of Sydney]. It was early morning and we were all half cut, not really taking matters seriously. After a short time of fooling around, things started to get serious and a message came through at about 2 a.m. from someone called Mary Fitton who said she'd been a courtier of Queen Elizabeth. We asked her a lot of stupid questions, such as how old would Prince Charles be when he came to the throne, and how many corgies the Queen owned, however she didn't seem to know anything about the Royal Court, and we dismissed her as a liar, and told her so.

A week later Bob McGuiness, one of the group said he had seen a ghost of Mary Fitton, who appeared naked at 2 a.m. and begged him to make love to her. Bob being his shy self declined. He should never have told us, because his life is not worth living, for we tease him relentlessly about the night he could have made love to one of the queen's handmaidens. The following poem is dedicated to Bob and Mary and is (we promise) the last time we will mention the matter ... (honest Robbo!).

This is the tale of Robbo's ghost (of which we hope you'll offer a toast);
He met her at a ouija party, and found her rather arty farty.
She said she'd lived with our London Queen, before she died, there was much she'd seen,
We gave her Gip and she left in a huff, but evidently that wasn't enough.
She fancied Robbo something bright, and came to his bed as a ghost one night,
Give me it Robbo she said with hot breath, but she frightened Robbo half to death.
Bob's days as a virgin are long gone, but sex with a ghost was just not on;
Though Mary showed him her sexy bush, our Bob wasn't ready for a royal flush.

Cowarts was fascinated for he realized that Bob McGuiness's friends' flippancy hid a greater truth. He immediately recognized that they had missed the main point in the story. Elizabeth was not the present queen as they had imagined, but Queen Elizabeth I.

No wonder Mary Fitton had known nothing of corgies of Prince Charles, for she was of a different era. Perhaps her appearance as a ghost was to enlighten 'Robbo' McGuiness. Could it be that he was the more serious of the group, seeing as his friends described him as being 'his shy self'. Perhaps his shyness was the exact reason why Mary Fitton appeared to him, in order to be taken seriously, though why, one might ask, would such a ghost attempt to seduce such a contact in this way? The story may very well have ended there – but events often take a strange turn, and the laws of synchronicity are difficult to explain...

Whilst researching a book, and looking for other ghost stories, Cowarts came across a book entitled *This Haunted Isle*. As he perused the book, he was amazed to read on page 106 the name Mary Fitton. Like a bolt of lightning the name jumped out of the page, and he realized that not only had he heard the name recently, but that it was the same person who had appeared as a ghost to Bob McGuiness, 12,000 miles away in Australia.

The book tells that Mary Fitton once lived in Gawsworth Hall, near Macclesfield, Cheshire. She was a charming and promiscuous 17-year-old who obtained great enjoyment through her position as a member of the court of Queen Elizabeth I. She evidently had a number of suitors, all much older than herself including Sir William Knolleys (Comptroller of the Queen's Household) and William Herbert who was imprisoned for fathering her child. She also later had two children to Sir Richard Leveson who, not legally married to her, considered her his '*Deare Sweet Wyff*'. In addition she gave birth to a child of Captain William Herbert and may well have been a lover of William Shakespeare himself who was said to 'have made her mortal'.

Despite her racy reputation and her strange haunting half a world away in Australia, her sightings in Britain are said to be very genteel. The ghost is reputed to walk on autumn evenings through the avenue of lime trees which stretch from the Harrington Arms to Gawsworth Hall. She is also said to haunt the old rectory and the local church. In recent years the owner of a Landrover had to brake violently in order to miss a walking hooded figure, and it is also recorded in *This Haunted Isle* that a sleeping odd job man was once disturbed by what was believed to be the ghost of Mary Fitton. Strangely the time of the haunting was 2 a.m., the exact time of her haunting in Australia, and the time when her spirit first came through to the modern world via a ouija board party, in that small flat 12,000 miles away.

6   The Ghost of the Sex-Crazed Cat

It was in the 1800s when Mr Edward Meynall, the nephew of Lord Halifax, and a keen collector of ghost stories, took great pleasure in repeatedly telling an extraordinary ghost story concerning a haunting by a sex crazed cat.

The incident which he told was thought to refer to himself, but on each occasion Meynall insisted that it was actually an account of a friend's experience.

Meynall states that the unnamed friend (let's refer to him as Edward Mayne), had taken a break with friends in Eastbourne in order to relax after a particularly long and arduous period of work which had resulted in him suffering from nights of restless sleep. Arriving at Eastbourne, he was surprised to find a party taking place, with a number of his close acquaintances being in attendance.

Edward immediately climbed the stairs in order to take the room which he normally occupied when in the house, and was surprised to be met on the landing by a cat which he had never seen before. The cat put on a show of great affection for the man, excitedly rubbing itself around his feet in such a manner that Mayne suddenly realized it was becoming sexually excited and was going through the motions of mating on his shoes. In addition it embarrassed him by whining strangely, and trying to climb his legs towards his genital area.

Desperately shaking free from the cat, he succeeded in reaching his room. Mayne managed with great difficulty to shut the cat out, and dressed for dinner, only to be met by the cat and its strange sexual behaviour once more as he walked back along the landing to the top of the stairs.

Edward was quite relieved as he descended the stairs to find that the cat did not follow him, and he hurriedly joined the other guests for a meal. When dinner was over, Mayne spoke to his host about the cat, and asked when he had obtained it, only to be told that he did not own a cat. The host explained that he did not like cats, though sometimes one of the cats from the neighbourhood came into the house of its own accord.

Edward Mayne dismissed the matter from his mind, only to have to confront the problems he had encountered earlier as he departed for bed. The cat once more began its excited show of affection on the landing, this time climbing beyond his waist, almost to his neck, before Mayne could detach it from his clothing.

During the following day, which was a Sunday, the cat continued its sexual onslaught on Mayne's shoes, whining hysterically and attempting to climb his clothing. However, each time the owner of the house tried to find the cat, it was nowhere to be found. That evening it was not on the landing and as Mayne retired for bed he thought that perhaps this time the feline nuisance had gone forever.

It was early in the morning when he awoke with a start. Something was pricking his body and he put his hand to his body to find something wet and warm there. Lighting a candle, Edward Mayne found that his nightshirt was covered in blood down one side of his body, and in his bed was the cat which had bothered him so much during the day. Mayne was outraged and with one swipe of his hand dashed the cat, which had either bitten or scratched him, to the floor. Instantly he felt the hair on the back of his neck stand up and a cold feeling of fear come over him. The angry cat hissed and spat with as much venom as it had shown sexual excitement earlier. Depending on which version of the story one wishes to believe, the cat now either vanished before his eyes, or alternatively began to speak, uttering obscene curses and blasphemies. Whichever is true, Edward Mayne bcame convinced that the cat was not of this world.

How the cat had got into the bed chamber remains a

mystery. According to one version of the tale, the cat had been let into the room by a servant, but a second version tells that the cat simply materialized of its own accord. Both versions tell of the marks being caused by the cat's attempt to suck a quantity of blood from his body, a task in which it succeeded and which left Mayne with furrowed tongue marks down the left side of his body.

Edward Mayne – despite his conviction that he had been attacked by a strange ghost in the form of a cat – evidently visited two doctors on his return to London to check that the wounds were not from a rabid animal. The doctors gave him the reassurance he sought and he evidently returned to a normal lifestyle, no doubt ensuring that he avoided the company of cats for the rest of his life.

7 The Wicked Spectres of Old Wallington

Situated on the B6342, approximately twenty miles or so north-west of Newcastle-upon-Tyne stands Wallington Hall, a seventeenth century building now under the protection of the National Trust. Local legend says that the previous building on the site was a haunt of rats, bats, and ghosts, and is featured in an ancient ghost book named *Fantasmes and Spectres in the North Country* by William Ramsey.

Though the book is not dated it refers to 'Old Wallington' as existing 'nigh on thirty years past', giving the book a rough publication date of 1715. Its style makes difficult reading as the book is printed in the old script where the letter 's' looks like an 'f'. It does however contain a number of weird ghostly stories. In particular, the strange story of 'Old Wallington' is of interest, and though clothed in the diplomatically social language of the time, gives a fairly graphic account of a series of sexual hauntings.

Let us hear the story in William Ramsey's own words:

Many of our Country Gentlemen in their busy hours apply themselves wholly to the chace, or to some other diversion which they find in field and wood. Not so the Country Gentlemen who lived around Old Wallington estate now gone and built upon once more in the wildest part of the North Country.

The posterity of the owner of this pyle which ceased to exist nigh on thirty years past, but partes of which do still exist there, was to hunt a set of creatures that punishment of deeds past had sent thither.

Should a spirit of superior or base rank, who is a stranger to these wilds, perchance to sleep in a particular publick chamber then all manner of spectres both human kind and abominable give mannifest offense.

Another who is very prolix in his Narrative writes me word that having ventured there whence he slept for a day or two, he was started by a gust of Wind that forced open his casement whence entered all manner of monsters enchanters and spirits all aflite and settling in his chamber. One was a young laughing Fop, another a Woman who stalked him as grave as a judge desireing free ingress and egress upon her.

Huzza'd out of his Seven Senses he suffered to be tempted beyond his strength and that base monster haunts him still. He labours under insupportable agonies yet.

The virgins of Great-Britain would best have killed a hundred lovers than sleep in Old Wallingtons tower. Its pretty chamber hangings and gilt leather for furniture with skreens and silky embroidery told nothing of the world of torment to be layed before them in sleep.

They indeed who did sink into sleep with their thoughts calm and innocent did but plunge themselves into scenes of Guilt and misery with Midnight Disquietudes for the satisfaction of Fantasms.

I think it has been observed in the Course of these papers that my manuscript gives not of names and though I long to speake out after the manner of the most celebrated authors of Great-Britain, Posterity would judge me harsh.

I was yesterday in a Coffee-House where I observed two persons in close conference over a Pipe of Tobacco. Having filled one for my own use and lit it from their wax-candle in the usual overture to conversation. Joining their company I saw that I had come together with a Fellow of my aquaintance, indeed the same one no less who wrote me of sleeping at Old Wallington. Though I would advise every other not to speak of such matters the conversation turned upon a raw Woman who had become a servant at Old Wallington. She was of a thin airy Shape and celebrated with pleasure the art of repeating often a visit from a winged fantasm while asleep and seated in an elbow-chair in her chamber.

Being clothed in a loose robe embroidered with figures of fiends and spectres she had fallen asleep; when on a sudden a thousand chimerical monsters beat at her casement and something wild appeared lifting her garment from her whence it hovered in the wind. I would give instances of all which happened in the name of Nox and Somnus but least to say the spectre took to the womans bosoms before beating its wings and providing its passion with many myriads of Disgrace upon her.

As we see many stars by the help of glasses may yet we not think it impossible there may be beings of substance which infinite space gives room to, which Gentlemen and the fair, being intellectual beings deserve of diversion over a bottle of wine...

It is interesting to note that the modern Wallington Hall has a 'ghost room' haunted by footsteps and noises in the night. It is credited with an 'atmosphere' and unidentified 'monsters' which flap their wings against the windows and wake up sleepers with heavy asthmatic breathing. Could it be that the mysterious 'set of creatures that punishment of deeds past had sent thither' still haunt the building which was built on the former site of 'Old Wallington'?

8 The Wicked Highwaywoman

Highwaymen have been said to haunt Britain's roads for hundreds of years, but few people outside Hertfordshire are aware of the ghost of the Highway*woman*, Catherine Ferrers.

Catherine is known locally as 'the wicked lady', and no wonder if tales of her sighting are to be believed. During her days as a 'highwayman', Catherine would ride a black horse and commit outrageous robberies. It is said that when she robbed an attractive gentleman, she would hold a pistol to his head whilst she ran her hand slowly, almost politely around every part of his body, starting at the face and finishing between the legs. It is said she gained delight from seeing the faces of the men, who naturally thought they were being fondled by another man. This wicked sense of humour was her trademark, and in recent years she is said to have appeared to a crowd gathered for a garden party, and delighted in the antics of the men, women, and children, who scattered in all directions at the sight of her.

Catherine seems to haunt both her old home of Markyate Cell and the lanes and roads around it. Sometimes she is actually seen, while at other times simply the beat of ghostly horses' hooves can be heard galloping past in the still night.

In 1840 a serious fire at her old home was blamed on her, and workmen who began to repair the building swore that they saw the ghost of a naked lady swinging from the branch of a tree during daylight hours. This kind of escapade is typical of the wicked sense of humour of Catherine Ferrers' ghost.

During her lifetime, Catherine Ferrers was a wealthy woman and had no need to rob. She is said to have married before she was twenty years old, and being of a flighty nature and bored with the humdrum world of a married lady, she began robbing coaches, purely for excitement. The goods she stole were kept with her outfit in a secret cupboard in a room above the kitchen at Markyate Cell.

Her most recent hauntings, though not numerous, are often of a playful sexual nature and always display her sense of humour. A courting couple, parked down a narrow country lane, reputedly had their underclothes dragged from the floor of their car, through the open window, and up into a tree by a gust of wind. It is said that the couple saw the ghost ride by, laughing at the antics of the half-naked man who had to climb the tree to retrieve the lost items.

Another couple were lying together on the grass in the area of Markyate House, engaged in nothing more serious than kissing, when it is said that buttons on both the man's shirt and the woman's blouse were snapped open (again by a sudden gust of wind), leaving the couple self-consciously trying to cover their embarrassment in front of the other people sitting nearby. One old man who had witnessed the display, and found it most amusing, said that although he had not seen the Wicked Lady on this occasion, the same thing had happened to himself forty years earlier. The ghost of Catherine Ferrers had ridden by, naked except for trousers and a hat, her laughing voice lingering long after she had disappeared.

It is said that this wicked but harmless and fun-loving woman died from injuries received whilst robbing the St Albans coach (though some say it was her lover who brought about her death). Whatever the true cause of her injuries, it is said that she arrived home mortally wounded, only to be buried by her husband in a secret tomb, hoping no doubt that her identity as a coach robber would be kept from the world.

No one is quite sure how the secret of her exploits leaked out, but one thing is for certain – Catherine Ferrers made it plain during her marriage that she was not prepared to spend her lifetime in boredom. In death too, her wicked earthy sense of humour continues to manifest itself, showing that a boring existence has once more been rejected by the Wicked Lady who now haunts the highways of Hertfordshire.

9   The Voyeuristic Wizard

Pendle Hill has a reputation as the haunt of witches, stretching back hundreds of years. Perhaps it is not surprising then that where witches are to be found so are wizards, though it is one wizard in particular (in ghostly form), who is renowned in the area of Alderley Edge, Cheshire. This particular ghost is well-known for his endless fascination for peeping on courting couples who use this peaceful area for their daytime romances. A number of couples have reported a naked, bearded man watching them from behind bushes, or disturbing their open-air lovemaking on a number of occasions. Though many may put the incidents down to local 'peeping-toms', others believe that the voyeur is the ghost of one of the ancient Pendle wizards.

One such wizard is commemorated in a verse to be found carved near a local well, and is further celebrated in the name of a nearby public house. The well water, which is said to flow as a result of the wizard's magic, was long renowned as promoting fertility in those who drank it. It is said that many childless young couples would drink the water before lovemaking in the hope that it would increase their chances of having a child.

The verse at the base of the well says:

> *Drink of this and take thy fill*
> *For the water flows by the wizard's will*

Though no one can tell when the first modern haunting took place, one tale is told of a young girl who told her parents that she had been watched by a naked little old man with a long white beard. Shortly afterwards, during the heat of summer, a young couple lay on the grass in the same area, kissing and showing their affection for each other. A naked old man with a long white beard came out of the bushes and startled them. Though he made no attempt to talk or touch the couple, he did walk close by them, suddenly vanishing into thin air.

Another sighting of the ghost was made by a retired police officer who was picnicking in the same area with his wife. After a short while they both felt they were being watched, and without drawing attention to the fact, they made a plan to grab hold of the offender. Thanks to his police training, the man was able to leave his wife eating her picnic lunch while he quietly encircled the area in order to come up behind the watching man without being observed.

Slowly creeping towards the area where the man had been spotted, the ex-policeman was surprised to find a naked old man, short in stature, and with long flowing white hair. Once within reaching distance, the ex-police officer rushed forward, ready to make a citizen's arrest. However, much to his amazement, the figure vanished before his eyes. How he explained the ghostly figure to his wife, let alone his ex-police colleagues, has never been revealed, though it is recorded that the couple spent their days out elsewhere from then on, and never picnicked in the area ever again.

10   The Marquis and the Radiant Boy

'Radiant Boys' (glowing childlike ghostly figures) are not an uncommon occurrence in the world of phantoms and spectres. Usually the appearance foretells a coming death as at Knebworth House (Herts), Chillington Castle and Corby Castle near Carlisle. However, during the eighteenth century, a similar appearance at an unnamed Irish stately home was said to materialize either with clothes or without, depending upon the sexual inclination of the person who beheld the frightening figure.

It is known that a number of homosexuals admitted to seeing this particular glowing naked boy, although they were always at pains to stress that their leanings were strictly for adult partners and not for children. After some time, guests simply refused to sleep in the room because of the possible consequences and the interpretations put upon any appearance of the ghost, and eventually, the owner told his servants that no guest should henceforth be accommodated in that particular chamber.

One particular tale of this ghost, said to come direct from the family of the second Marquis of Londonderry in the late 1700s, was told in a Victorian book entitled, *Ghost Stories* by Mrs Crowe. It was repeated in another book of that time, *Haunted Homes and Family Legends* by John H. Ingram. The same tale with a number of variations exists in a number of other publications.

The story tells of a Captain Stewart (later Lord Castlereagh), who when a young man, became lost during the pursuit of game whilst staying in Ireland. As the night drew in, Stewart realized that because of the atrocious weather conditions he would be unable to return home until the morning, and seeing the candles glowing in the rooms of a nearby country manor, made his way to the door to request accommodation for the night. Unfortunately, as was the way in those times, a number of similar stranded travellers had also requested to stay at the house overnight, causing some problems for the good-natured owner, who already had the house full of guests of his own.

Despite the lack of accommodation, the hospitable master of the house told his unannounced guest that he would find somewhere for him to sleep, though he would have to make do with a layer of blankets upon the floor. Thankful for small mercies, Stewart accepted, and was led away by the servant to join the other guests whilst preparations were found for somewhere for him to sleep.

The story in *Haunted Homes and Family Legends* tells us that:

Captain Stewart found the house crammed, and a jolly

party it was. His host invited him to stay, and promised him good shooting if he would prolong his visit a few days; and, in fine, he thought himself extremely fortunate to have fallen into such pleasant quarters.

Stewart was fortunate indeed. His bed was indeed a rather makeshift pile of rugs upon the floor but he was given his own room with a roaring peat fire. It mattered little to the man that the room was almost empty of furniture, for the rain beating at the shutters of the window reminded him of where he could have been sleeping if he had not come across the country house.

As he settled down to sleep, the enormous roaring fire crackled in the hearth, sending red-hot sparks up the chimney and occasionally out into the room. Fearing that his bedding might catch fire whilst he slept, Stewart dampened down the fire somewhat before stretching himself out and falling into a deep sleep.

The story continues:

> He believed he had slept about a couple of hours when he awoke suddenly, and was startled by such a vivid light in the room that he thought it was on fire; but on turning to look at the grate he saw the fire was out, though it was from the chimney the light proceeded. He sat up in bed, trying to discover what it was, when he perceived, gradually disclosing itself, the form of a beautiful naked boy, surrounded by dazzling radiance. The boy looked at him earnestly, and then the vision faded.

The captain was indignant at what he thought was a practical joke, and next morning at the breakfast table told his host in no uncertain manner, that although he was grateful in the extreme for his hospitality, he felt that the practical joke of the previous evening was uncalled for from a man of his standing. The host of course denied any knowledge of such a prank. He apologised for any misconduct and assured the captain that he would speak to each and every guest and servant until he found the culprit.

... one and all on their honour, denied the impeachment. Suddenly a thought seemed to strike him; he clapt his hand to his forehead, uttered an exclamation, and rang the bell. 'Hamilton', said he to the butler, 'where did Captain Stewart sleep the night?'

'Well, Sir,' replied the man, in an apologetic tone, 'you know every place was full – the gentlemen were lying on the floor three or four in a room – so I gave him the "Boy's Room"; but I lit a blazing fire to keep him from coming out.'

'You were very wrong,' said the host. 'You know I have positively forbidden you to put anyone there, and have taken the furniture out of the room to insure its not being occupied.'

Whether the country gentleman revealed to the future Lord Castlereagh the connection between the nakedness of the ghost and its reputed revelation of the sexual leanings of those that saw it is not revealed. The story does however go on to tell us that:

... he informed him gravely of the nature of the phenomenon he had seen ... that there existed a tradition in his family that whomever the Radiant Boy appeared to would rise to the summit of power, and when he had reached the climax, would die a violent death. 'And I must say,' he added, 'the records that have been kept of his appearance go to confirm this persuasion.'

It must be said that Robert Stewart (later Viscount Castlereagh) was not known to be homosexual, therefore at least one aspect of the legend of the 'Radiant Boy' appears to be at fault. He did however go on to become 2nd Marquess of Londonderry and a British statesman who held a number of important posts including Secretary for Ireland (1798–1800), Secretary for War (1805–1806 and 1807–1809) and Foreign Secretary (1812–1822). His rise to power had evidently been predicted correctly by the appearance of the naked ghost, as was his violent death (by suicide in 1822).

11 The Transvestite Valet

In the unlikely setting of Beverly Hills, USA, stood a private residence in the shape of a miniature English castle. Even more unlikely was the fact that this building once contained a real English ghost who is said to have travelled to America in 1945 with a genuine four-poster bed.

The original modern owner of the bed, Graham Donovan, was an Irishman involved in the antiques trade who had moved to America during the Second World War. Donovan quickly became wealthy and began to import large items of furniture, furniture collections, and even whole buildings, from Britain. During one of his trips to Britain just after the war, Donovan obtained possession of a four-poster bed which was said to have been slept in by a number of members of the British parliament during the 1700s. The antique dealer took a liking to the bed, imported it into America, and eventually had it placed in one of the bedrooms of his own house. Graham's wife Marion was an American sports shop owner's daughter and was aged about thirty-one when she first saw the ghost. Few other people sighted it, but its existence was confirmed by a succession of maids during their cleaning duties at that time.

Whilst Donovan was away on a business trip in Canada in 1947, his wife slept in the room alone except for her small dog which had a basket in the corner. During the night, the dog began growling and awakened Marion, who, thinking that someone had broken into the house, lay still, but with eyes open in an attempt to see whether anyone was in her bedroom. In the light of the bay window, where she had left her clothes draped across the back of a chair, she saw a faint movement of a slim male figure taking off his clothes. As she watched, the man slowly and sensuously began to put on her silky underclothing, starting with her knickers and bra, then sexily rubbing her expensive nylons slowly up and down his legs, and finally examining himself in the mirror as he did so.

Trying to fight off panic and staring in disbelief, Marion watched the man parade himself in her clothes, undress again, and replace his own clothes. His garments appeared strangely feminine, being loose-flowing and apparently made of brightly-coloured embroidered velvet. He finally put on a large feathered cap and walked towards the bed. Without looking down at the now terrified woman, the man once more began to take off his clothing, sighing as he did so. Terrified of being raped or worse, Donovan's wife lay rigid, as the man slowly pulled back the bedclothes to climb in. At this, Marion jumped out of bed and pulled the string of the light switch next to the bed, but was amazed to find no one there. Suspecting that it had all been a dream, the distraught woman walked over to check her frilly underwear which she had left on the back of the chair. She found that it had indeed been moved and now lay in an untidy heap on the floor next to the four-poster bed. It was then that the truth of the events dawned on her and she realized that she had seen a ghost.

Though shaken, she later told friends that she was fascinated by the fact that the bed she slept in was also shared by a transvestite ghost and on the second such haunting she did not even bother to switch on the light when the man climbed into her bed. Her curiosity to find out what his next move would be was never satisfied however, as he vanished immediately upon touching the sheets. The man appeared in her bedroom many times after that, always oblivious to the fact that he was being watched, although obviously fully aware of the female clothing which seemed to promote the haunting. It was usual for the ghost to appear when Mrs Donovan was sleeping alone in the room, but on one occasion her sister, taking her an early morning cup of tea, spotted it too. Thinking someone was hiding in the corner of the bedroom, she screamed and dropped the tray, only to find that Marion by this time used to the haunting, was rather amused by the incident.

Never did the mysterious figure speak, though it was occasionally heard to sigh. Neither was it known to visit other rooms in the house or wander further than six feet or so from the four-poster bed. The ghost's own clothing never altered throughout the period of the sightings, though various reports of the haunting have embellished reports of the colour or style of garments. All versions of the story state that the material worn was velvet (usually green), and the outfit included a feathered hat. Modern versions of the tale include many 'extras' never reported in the original story, such as a silver sword, goblets of wine, and even a female companion who would undress in front of male occupants of the bed. However, interesting as these descriptions are, their credibility is extremely suspect to say the least.

Maids cleaning the room described various sightings, and were said to have seen the figure wandering around in frilly underwear, or naked, getting in and out of bed. They were known to deliberately leave sexy underwear about in order to encourage the ghost to materialize, though all attempts at communicating with it resulted in it fading away before their eyes. Clothing which it had been wearing fell to the floor, obviously in a different place to that in which it had originally been placed. The ghost's style of dress was later described as that of an early seventeenth century valet, and it became affectionately known as *Valentine the Valet* to all of the housemaids. Donovan himself never saw the ghost, and was said to discourage talk of its existence, but his wife consulted a number of psychiatrists, mediums and even historians in order to try and discover the origins and motivations of the transvestite ghost. No one ever came up with a convincing explanation, and the bed with its ghost was destroyed along with much of the house during alterations to the property many years later. The new owner was evidently not aware of its existence.

Donovan died in 1977 and his wife eight years later. Shortly before her death she was confronted by a sceptical reporter concerning the details of the haunting in her previous home in Beverly Hills. Though pressed to deny the incidents ever happened, Marion's descriptions were so sincere and detailed that the reporter himself was completely convinced that the haunting had indeed taken place.

12 Granny's Wood Shed

Many people are asked 'what is the earliest thing you can remember?' Some can remember their third or fourth birthday party with ease, whilst others claim no positive memories until they were eight or nine.

Neil Straw, an only child, knows precisely the date and time of his first real memory, for it was 6 p.m. on a summer's day in 1952. It was Neil's seventh birthday party, and he was playing with his cousins at his grandma's home in Yorkshire. His grandparents had arranged the party as a treat, and though he has only vague fleeting memories of the party itself, he does remember a game of hide and seek which was timed to begin when the large clock in his grandparents living-room struck 6 o'clock.

The house was in a country area and though it was not a farm, sheds and outbuildings seemed to crowd an open plot of land round about, where chickens ran freely around the buildings. Neil ran off to hide and chose a rather large wood shed about 10 yards from the house. He clearly remembers opening the large wooden door and being instantly aware of the smell of sawdust and damp logs. As he lay there hiding and peeking through a crack in the wooden boards, he became aware of a noise in the far corner of the shed. Looking across he was surprised and shocked to see a naked man and woman rolling around and making noises on the floor.

Thinking that the man was hurting the woman, Neil ran from the shed and into the house, ignoring the 'blonk one two three' call of his cousin as he saw him dart towards the hide and seek base. Neil quickly told his uncle that a man was hurting a woman in the shed, and that he should go and help her. Neil's uncle dashed to the shed and slowly emerged, looking rather puzzled.

'Are you telling fibs Neil Straw'? he asked, pointing his finger accusingly.

'No, no,' Neil remembers himself saying, 'They had no clothes on … and he was rolling on top of her, and she was moaning.'

His uncle seemingly took it as a joke and quickly returned to the house, whilst Neil returned to the shed for another look.

Slowly opening the door, Neil stared into the gloom inside. He hadn't been telling lies! The couple were still there, though now she was laughing and giggling. Running as fast as his legs could carry him he arrived at the house once more, dragging his uncle by the hand back to the shed. Opening the door he was relieved to find the couple still rolling around in the corner.

'Look there,' he whispered, 'over in the corner.'

Neil's uncle looked to where he pointed. 'What?' he said. 'What are you pointing at?'

Neil couldn't believe it. Was his uncle blind? Couldn't he see the couple without clothes on, rolling in the corner? Couldn't he hear the noise the woman was making?

Neil's uncle stated he had had enough of these silly games, and without further ado, told Neil to go back to his cousins and to stop bothering him with his silly fibs.

The boy was outraged at being called a liar, especially as he considered it plain for anyone to see that he was telling the truth. Running back to the other children, he told them he had something to show them.

'Over in Granny's wood shed,' he said. His cousins dutifully followed him to the shed, and waited as he opened the large wooden door. Inside was ... NOTHING. Neil couldn't believe his eyes. Apart from logs, sawdust and a few tools there was nothing, and what's more, there was a large pile of unsawn tree branches where the couple had been rolling.

In later years Neil tried to make sense of what he had seen that day. With adult hindsight he now knew that the naked couple had been making love. However, he now questioned himself. He was unsure if the incident had ever really happened, or if the memory was nothing more than a half forgotten dream. Neil visited his uncle who was by now quite elderly and lived some miles away. No – he didn't remember the incident at all. The only memories he had of that party was that the kids had driven him round the bend with their noise and silly games. Neil reasoned that perhaps his uncle wouldn't have remembered. After all, to him it would have been only a fleeting moment when a nephew had told a tale and dragged him to an empty wood shed. Still, Neil was determined to find out if any of the other children remembered.

By now his cousins were dispersed around the globe. One in Australia, two in Scotland, and others he knew not where. Only two lived reasonably close, and though he had lost touch with them, he knew their addresses. Thumbing through his phone book he gave them a call. Helen (the daughter of the uncle he had taken to the shed), his eldest cousin, certainly remembered being taken with the others to the shed. She had been old enough at the time to guess what a naked couple might have been up to. David, the other relative, barely remembered the incident at all, but did confirm looking for something in the shed and being told by Neil that it wasn't there any more.

At least Neil was now satisfied that his childhood memory had not failed him, though he thought no more of the incident until his eyes caught the headlines of a local newspaper a year or so later: SHOPKEEPER CLAIMS STOREHOUSE HAUNTED BY NAKED COUPLE.

Thinking the story similar to his own childhood experience, he began to read the account of a shopkeeper on a new housing estate in the same town where he used to live. Having only been built six months, the owner had asked for a priest to be called in to exorcise his storeroom after a number of sightings of a ghostly naked couple frolicking on the floor. The address was 23 Moor-Park Road. This was coincidence indeed as his granny's house was also situated on Moor-Park Road (No. 2).

Neil took it upon himself to telephone the shopkeeper in order to compare notes and found the shopkeeper willing to talk and fascinated that two similar experiences should occur in the same street. Neil explained that his grandparents were Mr & Mrs Straw who had lived only doors away, and asked if the man was local and could remember them. After a stunned silence the shopkeeper spoke, saying that he did indeed remember them, as his parents had moved into one of the houses nearby when he was a lad. He said that Neil was obviously unaware that his grandparents' house had been knocked down along with the other two dwellings when the new estate was developed. The street had been renumbered and his shop had been built on the site of Mr & Mrs Straw's House. In fact his storehouse was on the exact site of the couple's old woodshed...

13   Naked Bald Agnes

Scotland's Holyrood House Palace is said to have been built following a hunt in 1128, when David I captured a stag by the horns as it chased him through the woods. The stag was but a ghostly image, though the horns remained, turning to a cross in David's hands. This is the first of many ghost stories associated with Holyrood House, whose name is said to mean 'Holy Cross House'. Mary Queen of Scots is said to haunt the building, as is her husband Lord Darnley, and her private secretary who was stabbed to death by her husband.

The grounds are also reputedly haunted by a naked ghost, which was recorded often in years gone by, but which seems to appear less often in modern times, and whose image now appears to be fading at each and every haunting. A ghost which has become known to many by the appellation 'Naked Bald Agnes'. Though not indulging in any form of sexual activity, the ghost of Agnes Sampson has historical sexual origins, and is surely one of the strangest examples of naked ghosts which haunt Britain today.

In her day Agnes Sampson was a well-known woman of gentility who was tried for witchcraft by Scotland's King James VI in 1592. Though initially denying all charges, under torture she began to admit to working with other witches to raise up a storm in order to sink a ship carrying King James to Denmark. The politically biased trial ended in her conviction based solely on her own confessions given under torture, including the incredible tale that she and her friends had taken to sea in sieves in order to work their magic spells. During her torture, Agnes suffered the humility of being stripped naked and having every hair shaved from her body. In addition she was subjected to the agony of burns from ropes, purposely pulled across her face and bare breasts. She also suffered the pain of a 'witches bridle' which pierced her cheeks and tongue with sharp spikes, and was fastened by spiked iron straps to the wall of her cell.

The sadistic and sometimes sexual torture inflicted on Agnes Sampson and her supposed cohorts was intended of course to bring forth confessions. There is no doubt that it succeeded in bringing about the required result in virtually all such cases. It is believed by many students of the subject that such suffering may very well result in a psychic image being somehow locked within time. Because of its intensity these images are still capable of being observed as ghosts by those sensitive to such feelings, right up to the present day.

There are many who have claimed to see Agnes Sampson's ghost. Some say she drifts across the lawn of Holyrood House dressed in a white shroud, whilst others tell of a more bizarre haunting concerning a smooth white naked woman. Many reports were given in the nineteenth century of the sighting of a bald naked lady, without eyebrows or other body hair. She makes no sound and no movement but simply stands silently without expression for only a few minutes before slowly vanishing into thin air as quickly as she appeared. This they believe is Agnes Sampson's image, a sad ghost of a tortured soul, whose only crime was to be caught up in the political bickering of her own time, and who suffered untold mental agonies at the hands of her sexually sadistic torturers.

14   Ghosts of Mermaids

The gentle ghosts which once haunted the northern isles of Scotland, were said to be the earthly forms of mermaids and mermen. It is said that they desired sex with the humans who lived on the islands, and would take on a spiritual body in order to get it.

One such haunting was said to have affected a whole village in the late eighteenth century. The unnamed community of twenty or so families was supposedly visited by a group of mer-people who had changed themselves into human form during the previous evening. The group introduced themselves as a group of missionaries and offered to pay for a celebration in the village that evening, where drink was said to flow freely. When all of the older local villagers fell into a drunken stupor, the mermen and mermaids chose the most beautiful young women and most handsome young men as sexual partners, and retired to bed with them. After sexual intercourse had taken place, the mer-people were said to lose their human form, fading away to ghostly images which were still able to converse with their partners. At this they revealed themselves as people of the sea, proving their identity by showing their webbed toes and fingers. They then gently kissed their partners, telling them that they were grieved to leave, and promising to protect the islanders and their children from all hazards of the sea. With tears in their eyes, the mer-people faded completely from sight, leaving the islanders equally distressed at the loss of their newfound loves.

Another haunting in the late 1800s was told by a fisherman who lived alone in a fisherman's bothy at the

side of a loch close to Oban in Scotland. The fisherman was almost a recluse, but was considered to be a seer and a wiseman by those he did come in contact with. This reputation was based on nothing more substantial than the birthmark of a cross over the man's right eye. Though the man considered himself nothing more than a local fisherman, he did encourage the belief in his powers as it provided another method of income to supplement his meagre existence.

The bothy (tiny cottage) was built in an isolated spot close to the water's edge. The building was not accessible by road, and was the haunt of all kinds of wildlife such as otters and seals which swam around unconcerned by the activities of the fisherman who would talk to them as friends. One winter's evening when the door of the bothy had been closed for days to keep out the wind, the fisherman was surprised to hear a knocking. Opening the door he found a young girl of about eighteen years of age, soaking wet, who asked for shelter. The girl told a remarkable tale of having swum the freezing cold waters of the loch from a nearby island, in order to find food for her dying mother. The fisherman allowed her to stay the evening and soon noticed her webbed fingers as she warmed her hands by the fire. He promised her dried fish to take to her home, and said he would row her back in the morning. The girl thanked the fisherman but said that she must return that same night. The fisherman insisted that the rowing boat would not survive crossing the loch in the heavy waves of the storm which was now raging outside. At this the girl smiled sweetly and fell asleep by the fire.

During that same evening the fisherman awoke to find the warm sensation of the girl's body next to his own. Before long the couple were making love, after which they both sat by the fire in silence. To the fisherman's amazement the girl began quickly to fade before his eyes, a state which continued until she seemed merely to be a faint ghostly image. The girl sadly told the man of her true identity – that she was a sea creature in human form. She apologised for misleading the fisherman, explaining that her mother (also a sea creature) was indeed dying, and that she had told her daughter to mate with a human in order to provide her with a grandchild before her death. The child would take the form of a seal who would be sent to visit the fisherman in the summer. With this she vanished completely, never more to return.

The summer came, and the fisherman, now believing he had experienced only a dream, watched the newborn seals sunning themselves on the rocks around his bothy. He talked to them as he always did, jokingly asking which was his son. To his astonishment a young seal pup jumped into the water and submerged, only to raise its head close to the side of his rowing boat. The fisherman was struck dumb with amazement, for over its right eye, the seal sported a birthmark like his own in the shape of a large cross…

Such hauntings were said to be a regular event in days gone by, and similar legends still exist. These now refer to the 'Selkie Folk who live as seals for most of the year, but resume their human form on Midsummer's Eve.

It is said that those who are descended from these ghostly couplings can still be found on the islands today.

They are said to retain the characteristics of their forefathers and are distinguishable by their webbed feet or fingers, or by horny scales on their hands or soles of their feet.

15 The Heavy Breather of Heathrow

Surprisingly, airports are often said to be frequented by ghosts, although usually of the First World War aerodrome variety, where phantom dead airmen are reputed to walk across the tarmac at night, or to be found wandering the disused buildings. Modern airports too however, are reputed to have their hauntings, including London's Heathrow, which boasts no less than five separate ghosts, one of which is reputed to have a liking for ladies in low necklines. The 'heavy breather' as it has become known has never actually been seen, though its orgasmic breathing has been heard on a number of occasions, particularly by airport staff. It would seem that it is 'turned on' by women in uniform, particularly those with rather large bustlines and loose-fitting tops.

It is not recorded when the first occurrence took place, and though a number of theories have been put forward with regard to who the heavy breathing ghost is, a number of people have suggested that perhaps a highwayman (possibly even 'Dick' Turpin) haunts the area, for the airport is built upon Hounslow Heath which was once a well-known haunt of highwaymen and robbers.

One such haunting happened in July 1988 when an employee of Pan American airways was alone in the ladies' where she was changing her air hostess uniform. As she undid her top and stripped down to her bra, she became aware of the sound of breathing somewhere behind her. Though she knew she was alone in the room the young woman instinctively looked round, but unable to see anything, continued to undress. She noticed that the breathing was getting louder and quicker, and became unnerved as she sensed the sound was getting closer and closer (almost as if it was emanating from an unseen face which was looking over her shoulder). Thinking that perhaps her colleagues had concealed a tape recorder somewhere in the restroom as a joke, she continued, trying not to show the cold fear which was building up inside her. It was only when the breathing reached orgasmic proportions that she grabbed her clothes together and fled the room in a blind panic.

On a second occasion, another employee of Pan American airlines was panicked into running from the staff car park after being 'chased' by animal-like breathing which grew closer and closer until once again it seemed to be hovering over her shoulder, almost as if someone were looking down the low neckline of her dress from behind. Once again the ghost was invisible, but no less terrifying because of this.

Another airport employee, this time a male engineer, was reported to have been sitting on the toilet when he became conscious of the feeling that he was not alone in the cubicle. Telling himself that he was being irrational, he wilfully continued to sit there for a full five minutes, despite hearing the sound of heavy breathing all around him. He later denied to workmates that he had been another victim of the heavy breathing ghost, yet despite this he henceforth refused to use the works' toilet. Indeed, from the day of the incident to the time he left the airport's employ, he would not even enter the building in which the toilet block was situated.

This would appear to be the only case of a male being haunted by this particular ghost, though a number of women have told similar tales of the sound of panting, wheezing and heavy breathing, giving the impression of someone in sexual arousal, actually looking down their low necklines from behind.

In a strange variation on the theme, a young woman working at one of the ticket desks told how she had come across the heavy breathing ghost under different circumstances. It would seem that during a particularly busy period on the desk, she became aware of what she thought was a dog sniffing around her feet whilst she was in the middle of dealing with a customer. Looking down she could see nothing, and though she tried not to give any indication to the person she was dealing with at the other side of the desk, the airport employee felt that the dog (as she thought it to be at the time) was between her feet, looking up at her. Instinctively she repeatedly kicked out with her foot, hoping to drive the animal away. This only resulted in an increase in the volume of the noises coming from down below (which by now had become almost gasping in intensity). The customer who had been polite and proper throughout, gave a wry smile. 'I don't know who you've got behind that desk,' he said, 'but he sure sounds as though he can't wait for you to finish work.' With this he picked up his tickets and walked away, leaving the ruffled, confused and embarrassed ticket clerk to cope with the long queue of amused customers.

16 The Mooner of Romney Marsh

'Mooning', the dubious art of baring one's bottom to the view of strangers is usually considered to be a modern activity, often associated with the drunken occupants of football coaches tearing down Britain's motorways or bored rebellious youths who want to shock their elders. However, there is at least one recorded case of 'mooning' taking place on a number of occasions in the early 1800s, on Romney Marsh in Kent, as well as in Camber and Winchelsea to the south-east. The 'mooner' was a ghostly figure, said to dress 'in the manner of a gamekeeper but with a tricorn hat and a hunting horn by his side'.

The sightings of this misty figure occurred over a wide area of Romney Marsh between the years 1801 and 1833 (when a priest was said to have exorcised the ghost in an open air ceremony 'in order that the fairer sex and gentlemen of gentility should not anymore have their senses outraged by the base and defiled spirit').

The first mention of a sighting of the ghost was close to St Mary in the Marsh in 1801, when a group of three young men who were said to have been carrying smuggled goods inland from the coast, stopped to meet others who were to purchase the goods from them. As they sat in the mist smoking their clay pipes, a figure emerged from the darkness. Thinking that this was their contact, the men spoke to the strange figure who continued to walk past them without a word. This did not surprise the smugglers, who assumed that the man was simply being quiet in order to avoid detection. In single file they unconcernedly followed the man into a group of bushes close by. In the light of their lanterns they were amazed to see the man remove his breeches, squat down in front of them and reveal his bare bottom. At this the figure vanished completely, and despite a prolonged search, no trace was found of him. When their real contacts did eventually arrive, they were said to be extremely amused by the tale, and within a short while the events of the night were the talking point in taverns throughout the area.

In 1809 a number of sightings were made in daylight over a large area of the marshes. Travellers by horse and by coach reported seeing a figure with a tricorn hat and hunting horn who would squat down in front of them and ' ... reveal his naked nether quarters in a most distressing way'. On each occasion the ghost vanished immediately without trace, and the haunting was over within two or three minutes of the man first being sighted.

A young woman named Marion Bonnington who was out riding near Hamstreet in 1832 gave perhaps the most graphic description of the ghost in a candid letter to her mother in Sevenoaks:

… it was the most extraordinary event of my life, and one which I pray I shall never have to experience again. As I passed along the dirt-track I noticed a rather scruffy fellow walking some distance ahead who seemed not to have heard me approaching. As I came upon him I shouted (so that I would not run him into the ditch), for Blaise [her horse] was travelling at quite a pace. In the event it was necessary for me to slow down to almost a stop as I perceived the old man must be deaf. As I came upon him I saw he was dressed rather strangely in old shiny leather clothes and a pointed hat like the one papa used to keep in the box in the garret. As he half turned (not to look at me but to see something to his right), I perceived a flower or garland sticking from a drinking horn on his chest. His countenance was that of a rough fellow and it quite made the short hair on my neck stand on end, and I became quite cold as if the weather had suddenly taken on the feel of a winter's day. As I understood him to be deaf, and not wishing now to pass him, I held Blaise back with the intention of turning her for home, when suddenly the man (though I would not call him that now) bent low and quickly dropped his leggings. Though I know you may laugh wickedly at what I am about to reveal, I was most fearful at that moment, for he then went on to display his bare cheeks and tailpiece between. I was at once shocked, fearful and amused (for I still did not think he knew I was there), and I was quite unsure what I should do next, however as I looked upon him, the fellow faded (looking somewhat of the texture of a counterpane), before vanishing completely in front of my eyes. I then grew so cold with fright that it was all I could do to kick Blaise (who seemed fully unaware of this fantasm) into a gallop. Though you know I would not lie to you mama, I well understand any disbelief you may show, however on arriving back at the village, I was asked by Mrs Hothfield of my distress. She said I looked as though I had seen a ghost and upon being told of what I had seen (though of course I did not wish to reveal that he had dropped his leggings) she herself asked if he had in her own words, untagged his breeches. Upon my revealing that this was so she informed me that I had seen an apparition who commonly haunts the marshes and begged me pay no heed as she said he was harmless. Mrs Hothfield talks as if the experience is commonplace and revealed to me that her own husband once saw the same apparition twice whilst out walking two years ago ...

The young lady goes on to say that she will reveal even more details when next she sees her mother. One wonders what additional facts were to be told concerning the strange ghost.

There are many factors with regards to this particular haunting which appear not to readily conform to the usual pattern of events. The ghost appeared both to groups of people and to solitary figures also. Though its actions were repetitive in nature, the hauntings covered a remarkably wide area of the Romney Marshes. It did not appear to be aware of those who saw it, yet why then did it drop its trousers and reveal its bottom to them?

The figure was seen both from the rear and from the side, but it would appear never from the front, and on only one occasion are we given any description of its facial features. Added to this is the fact that it was seen both during the day and at night, by male and female observers alike, and for a relatively short period (as hauntings go), of thirty-two years. Why, one might ask, was it dressed 'like a gamekeeper'? And what was the significance (if any) of the flower in its drinking or hunting horn?

Finally one wonders why the length of this particular haunting lasted only a short while, the man seemingly appearing and disappearing straight after the 'mooning'.

Unfortunately, unless science is able to provide the key to strange hauntings such as this, it would seem we are never to know the answers to any of these questions. One hesitates in this case to ask the question, 'Shall we ever get to the *bottom* of it all?'

17 The Spectre That Saved a City

Around the early 1600s, Bolling Hall (near Bradford) came into the possession of Richard Tempest, a sturdy supporter of King Charles I and the royalist cause in general. Following the defeat of the Roundheads at the Battle of Adwalton Moor, the royalist commander (the Earl of Newcastle) took the hall as his headquarters and began what later became known as 'the second siege of Bradford'. Using the hills around Bradford as his military standpoint the earl opened heavy fire on the city which was being defended with muskets by Sir Thomas Fairfax. The story goes that the siege quickly took its toll, and Fairfax, finding himself left with only a single barrel of powder, but not a single match to light it with, surrendered the town to the Earl of Newcastle.

Newcastle was obviously delighted with the quick results of his military tactics, yet was said not to have been a man of mercy. Panic spread through the population of Bradford as rumours spread that the earl had made a vow before the end of the battle, that if he should be successful in taking Bradford he would order his troops to massacre all men, women and children as recompense for the loss of the life of the Earl of Newport, who was said to have been barbarously butchered by the people of the city during the first siege.

The dreaded massacre never took place, and though many in the city gave thanks to God for the Earl of Newcastle's change of heart, none were aware of the strange happening which had prompted the aristocrat's decision.

During the evening prior to the Earl of Newcastle's victory, the man had retired footsore and weary to his bed at Bolling Hall. His chamber (even at that time) was known as the ghost room, and was reputedly haunted by a woman in white who would quietly wander the building, never making a sound. Guests would be startled by her appearance at unusual times, but were never frightened as she was not known to have done anyone harm (in fact, quite the contrary). Rumour had it that the lady in white protected the building and its occupants, and that those who saw her could sleep safely in their beds, knowing full well that her appearance signalled an assurance of her personal protection.

The earl was past caring about 'silly ghost stories' and having taken a number of brandies to assist with his sleep, and no doubt to ease his conscience regarding the planned massacre of Bradford's citizens, he quickly sank into a deep slumber.

Had the hauntings that followed been 'run of the mill', then perhaps the slaying of thousands of men, women, and children would have taken place, and the pages of the history books would tell a different story. As it was, it appeared that the gentle and protective 'woman in white' of Bolling Hall would show that she was prepared to go to any lengths in order to save the inhabitants of the city, even if it meant breaking her years of self-imposed silence in order to plead for their lives. As we shall see, it transpired that she was actually prepared to go further, by offering her feminine charms as an incentive for the Earl of Newcastle to change his mind.

Immediately after the event, many scoffed at the reason given by the earl for changing his mind with regard to the planned revenge killing of Bradford's citizens, accusing the aristocrat of suffering from the effects of too much brandy. Many however, believe his account of what took place in the 'ghost room' that night, for it is well-known that up until his experience the earl had been extremely sceptical of the existence of ghosts. Over the years, tales have become exaggerated and confused concerning the events that took place, but at least two versions of the story state that the earl spoke of four separate visits to his bed-chamber that night by the 'white lady'.

On the first occasion the ghost had simply walked into his room, making no noise, and leaving him wondering if in fact he had seen her at all. Later, disturbed by a scratching of rats or mice under his bed, the earl had once more opened his eyes to see the same figure at the bottom of the four-poster bed. As he tried to come to his senses, and to his great amazement, the spectre of the white lady opened her mouth and spoke, saying, 'Pity poor Bradford', upon which she vanished as quickly as she had materialized.

By now the earl was quite alarmed by what had taken place, and attempted to stay awake. Despite his efforts he did drift off into sleep, only to be woken about an hour later by the feel of his bedlinen being pulled from him by the ghostly hands of the white lady who again pleaded 'Pity poor Bradford'. The hair on his neck standing on end, the terrified earl jumped from his bed, shouting at the image to 'leave me be … leave me in peace'. With this the ghost once more implored him to 'Pity poor Bradford' before fading away in front of his eyes.

Collecting his senses together, the earl resolved out loud that the decision had been made, and that nothing would now make him change his mind. But the persistent ghost was not to be outdone. Her last visit to his bed-chamber came about an hour before dawn when the earl was subjected once more to the bedlinen being drawn from his body. This time he was even more terrified to see the ghostly figure completely naked, and attempting to climb upon the bed beside him, all the time whispering and pleading continuously, 'Pity poor Bradford, pity poor Bradford, pity poor Bradford ... ', and obviously willing to offer her body as an inducement for the trembling earl to change his mind.

Whether he was overcome by shame or whether he was moved to emotion by the lady sacrificing her chaste ghostly body in order to save others is not known, but it is said that the aristocrat broke down in tears and promised that neither man, woman, nor child would be harmed by his soldiers. With this the ghost smiled sweetly, nodding a silent thank you, and evaporated into thin air.

The following morning the commander gave orders that the citizens of Bradford should be spared, and that furthermore the town should be given over to the people.

Many theories exist concerning the spectre that saved the people of Bradford. Some say the hauntings were the result of a troubled conscience, whilst others argue that the whole episode was a drunken dream. A third school of thought insists that what the earl saw was a local bar-wench who was given the job of persuading him to change his mind.

Despite all the many explanations, and the fact that there was no doubt in the minds of many that the earl was troubled by his conscience, it is argued that the commander would be unlikely to be so drunk on the eve of such an important potential victory. To his dying day the earl swore that his decision was the result of the pleadings of the ghostly figure, and further evidence is given to support the truth of the whole episode by the fact that the room in which he slept was already known to be haunted by the protective 'white lady'.

Today Bolling Hall is still haunted by the lady (now known as the Grey Lady). It would seem that over the years her whiteness has faded to a misty grey, and that time has dimmed the image (but certainly not the reputation) of perhaps the only ghost in history who is known to have been prepared to prostitute her body in order to save the population of a city from death at the hands of a merciless enemy.

18 Archibald's Orgy in Hell

Around the 1700s, the city of Glasgow was the location of a group of well-to-do ladies and gentlemen of disreputable character who had organized themselves into a group known as the 'Hell Club'. Though having no connection with the later world-famous 'Hell Fire Club' in England, the activities of its members were likewise of a dubious nature.

It was well-known in the 'right circles' that within this group you would find 'drunkenness, sexual freedom and blasphemy'. Each evening a select group would meet to carry out its sexual excesses, whilst weekly the whole club would gather to take part in sexual orgies of the wildest nature. A yearly 'Saturnalia' was held each New Year when new members would be recruited and when a certain amount of mild loosening of moral behaviour was generally accepted by all.

The leader of this Glasgow Hell Club was only ever referred to by his Christian name of Archibald. He was known by all to be the most liberal and outrageous member of the club, and was well known for repeating loudly and often his ambition to 'F..k in Hell', a habit which strangely appeared to act as a magnet to otherwise prim and proper ladies, consequently attracting a lot of new women recruits to his licentious circle of friends in the club.

Following one of the annual Saturnalia festivals celebrated at the club, Archibald failed to attend the next usual nightly gathering. The man had never been known to miss such a meeting. However, in his place was a handwritten note, apologizing for his absence and saying he was to resign and would attend no more. No explanation was given for this strange turn of events and a number of the club's élite consequently called upon him to enquire into the circumstances leading up to his resignation from the club.

Archibald, at first reluctant to give an explanation, was eventually pressed and cajoled into revealing what had happened to him following the annual Saturnalia. The drunken reveller had been driving home when his private coach was stopped by a ghostly apparition in black. The ghost had explained that since Archibald was interested in matters of the flesh, and had expressed on a number of occasions his ambition to 'F..k in Hell', he was to be given the chance to realize his ambition. At this his horse reared violently, dashing Archibald unconscious to the floor.

Almost immediately the man was aware of leaving his own body as if he himself were a ghost. He described the sight of his earthly body lying without movement in the wet leaves at the side of the country road, whilst his 'spiritual' body got up and dusted itself down. Archibald assured his friends that such was the sensation, he was sure in his own mind he was dead. His companion in black however, sensing his feelings, assured him that all was well, and that he would return to the land of the living soon.

'In the meantime,' he said, 'follow me.'

Still looking behind him at his own body lying in the gutter, he was very much aware that the horses sensed his 'spiritual' presence as he walked past them in pursuit of the dark ghostly stranger.

'Where are we going?' inquired Archibald.

'To Hell,' was the curt reply. 'To Hell…'.

Archibald followed silently into the darkness of the lane until slowly he was no longer aware of the fields and trees around him, but seemed to be in a misty black tunnel which eventually ended at a large wooden door. The black-cloaked figure knocked and bolts rattled as the ghostly figure told Archibald that this was the hell he had always wanted to visit.

The door creaked open and to Archibald's surprise there

was not a sign of fire, brimstone, or any of the other dreaded consequences he expected. Instead a bright searing light hit his eyes, together with the sounds of music and laughter. He could also hear the familiar moans and groans of sexual activity.

A scene of utter debauchery met his eyes. Couples and groups frolicked everywhere in sexual abandon. Others staggered around singing in a drunken daze. Swearing and blasphemy uttered from the mouths of those in sexual embraces, whilst both male and female hands groped at his body as he passed through the seething masses.

Amongst those engaged in sexual activity was a former female member of the Hell Club, coyly referred to in Victorian accounts as the well-known Mrs D. She happened to be the pretty young wife of a famous Scottish surgeon. Mrs D. was evidently known by Archibald to be dead, and he bid her rest from her activity so that he could gather an account of her life after death.

'Rest?' cried Mrs D. 'Rest …? There is no rest in Hell,' at which she continued with her activity with her partner. The man was grey-haired and wizen-faced and appeared to be well over eighty years of age.

As he looked around Archibald could now see the extent of the sexual licence which was taking place. Men and women with animals, very old with the very young, and undescribable acts of sexual sadism and masochism. Even Archibald was disgusted.

The black figure spoke. 'Now is your chance; pick your pleasure and f..k in hell.'

Archibald declined crying, 'Take me back … take me back from this wicked place.' The cloaked figure replied, 'Very well but carry on your revelling and you shall return within a year and a day.'

The mysterious ghostly figure immediately returned back towards the door, picking its way through the naked bodies upon the floor, with Archibald following close behind. Closing the door behind them, Archibald soon found himself back at his coach where his body was still lying in the wet leaves as it had been when he left it. Within seconds he was aware of 'entering his body' and his earthly body stirred into life. Picking himself up, he once more climbed into the coachman's seat and with a pull on the reins he drove home somewhat dazed, reflecting on his strange experience.

In the night that followed, he thought long and hard upon his experience. Though he put the events down to hallucinations through the effects of heavy drink coupled with the fall from his coach, Archibald was still vividly able to recall all that had happened. Reluctantly he had decided to take no chances, and consequently wrote his note of resignation to the Hell Club.

On hearing his explanation, his friends laughed loudly at his gullibility. Indeed, it had only been a vivid dream brought about by the fall, they reasoned. Joining in the good-natured laughter of his friends, and feeling slightly ridiculous, Archibald relented. Throwing on his coat and cloak, he took up their suggestion to forget all about the incident, and followed them down to the club.

Within no time Archibald had resumed his old practices, though it was noticeable that he no longer uttered the previously commonly uttered phrase concerning his ambition with regards to his desired activities in hell.

A year passed and the annual Saturnalia festival came round once more. Archibald was acutely aware that it was now a year and a day since his 'hallucination' had been experienced. Friends joked with him saying that he had proved fate wrong, for he had neither changed his drinking ways, nor made any efforts to cut down on his beloved debauchery. Archibald sat nervously drinking heavily in order to forget the event of the previous year, and taking little part in the sexual activity going on around him.

By the time the Hogmanay party was over and the first light of dawn was creeping over the skyline, Archibald could hardly stand. The last remaining hangers-on from the debauchery of the previous evening assisted him to his horse in the stables nearby, and with a mumbled farewell, Archibald set his horse for home.

The same friends, now partly sobered, left the club a

number of hours later. As they travelled from the city towards Archibald's home, they found his old horse quietly grazing by the side of the road. A little further on lay the body of their friend. Archibald appeared to have fallen face down onto the road, his body partly submerged in a shallow ditch of wet leaves.

Help was sought and Archibald's body was taken home by coach, whilst much talk was made of his supposed experience of the previous year. Many members agreed that the ghostly experience had actually taken place, whilst there were those who put the whole episode down to sheer coincidence.

Whatever the truth of the matter, it would appear that the activities of the Glasgow Hell Club went on as normal for some years, and it is even said that the club from that time onwards celebrated a special event on the day following the Saturnalia festival. The day became not only a memorial of a well-loved friend, but also a special celebration of the day that Archibald entered death, and in having done so, achieved his one ambition in life.

19   The Glowing Nudes

The sudden appearance of a naked adult male to a young girl can be deeply disturbing, more so if the girl has lived a sheltered life in a relatively isolated part of the country. Imagine then the feelings of three young sisters when confronted by the sight of a number of male naked ghosts who crossed their path whilst on their way home from a friend's house near Morland in Westmorland.

Having spent the evening with friends, the three sisters were walking towards home in a region known locally as Skellaw Wark, when they were startled by the tall figure of a man emerging in front of them. The man was completely naked and glowed with a strange yellow-green light which at first must have made the girls imagine they had come in contact with an alien life form.

The ghostly figure walked across their path to a nearby rock, stopped, raised its fist threateningly and then vanished into the ground. Looking at each other with amazement, the girls stood and grasped each other's hands for reassurance. However, before they had come to their senses enough to speak, they witnessed a second (but different) naked and glowing ghostly figure emerging from the same spot. This figure too crossed their path, lifted its fist, and then as before, sank slowly into the ground.

Though taken aback by the strangeness of the figures, and the sight of naked genitals, the girls had the presence of mind to begin counting, as a continuous stream of these strange glowing ghosts went through the same motions as their predecessors. Finally the eleventh and last figure vanished into the earth.

Terrified, the girls ran all the way home, desperately trying to convince their mother of what they had seen and of the events that had actually taken place.

Many years later an investigation found that in 1827 eleven human skeletons, said to have laid on the spot for over a thousand years, had been unearthed at Skellaw Wark. The skeletons were all said to have had a gold bangle on their wrist (which was removed before the bones were reburied or otherwise disposed of).

Though one question had possibly been answered regarding the angry fist waving of the ghosts (no doubt to show their disapproval of the removal of their bangles), investigators have yet to explain the second and most unusual feature of this particular haunting – that is, their glowing yellow-green bodies. Further instances of the haunting are not recorded – perhaps what had happened was that simply by chance the sisters had witnessed the final ghostly procession of the souls of the eleven skeletons which had been earlier exhumed and robbed of their precious golden bracelets.

20   A Sight For Sore Eyes

It was a winter's evening in 1971 when Marc Fardon, a college student, was alone in the college library reading from textbooks and preparing for his exams. As he read, his tired eyes were distracted by something which seemed to move behind the row of bookcases in front of him. Getting up to investigate he was startled to come across an attractive young woman dressed only in a very skimpy modern négligé. The girl who looked quite 'solid', smiled at Fardon, whispered a single word, 'sexy', and then quickly vanished through the solid row of books.

Fardon immediately finished his studying, thinking that perhaps he had been overdoing things, and went back to his room to mull over the strange experience. Feeling rather foolish, Fardon told his room-mate what had happened, and having exchanged a few jokes the pair went out for the evening, forgetting all about the incident.

Returning at about 11 p.m., the pair found their room in a ransacked state. Books were thrown everywhere and clothes were scattered as though caught up in a whirlwind. Thieves were suspected, but nothing appeared to be missing, and no visible signs of forced entry could be found.

Fardon told his room-mate that he would go and report the matter, and left quickly by way of a long corridor leading to the stairs. As he approached the stairwell he was startled by a figure which seemed to have appeared from nowhere and was now standing halfway down the stairs looking up at him. Continuing on his way, it was not long before he recognized the same young woman whom he had encountered in the library earlier in the evening, though this time her négligé was unfastened leaving nothing to the imagination. Fardon stopped in anticipation, waiting for the 'solid and real looking figure' to vanish, which she did within seconds, after smiling and teasingly displaying her seductive body.

In a blind panic the young student ran back up the steps three at a time and began charging along the passageway, only to find his room-mate running towards him in the opposite direction.

'Marc ... Marc,' he cried in panic, 'you're not going to believe what's just happened to me ...'

Both young men returned to the room which by now was tidy and in order. Fardon's room-mate explained that as soon as Fardon had left the room 'all hell broke out'. Clothes had started swirling round the room and books had flown to the bookshelf of their own accord. The experience was described as 'like watching a movie in reverse'. Everything that had been thrown around the room had returned of its own accord to its original tidy position.

Though neither could explain what was happening, both realized that the apparently tidy poltergeist and the lady in the négligé must have some connection. Over the next few days they began tracing the history of the room to try to find records of either a student committing suicide there or any other similar stories which might have relevance to the strange events. Strangely nothing was found, and even attempts at contacting the sexily-clad ghost by ouija board and spirit mediums drew a blank, until finally time passed and the pair almost forgot about their strange experiences. After graduating, they lost contact with each other.

A number of years later the two former students met by complete accident whilst attending a conference in London. It was inevitable that the pair should begin to discuss the haunting and Fardon told his former room-mate that there was something he had not told him at the time of the events. His friend was intrigued and asked what it was.

'Well,' he said, 'I didn't want to frighten you, but the girl in the négligé spoke to me. She said that her name was Ann Kerenof and that she was going to get you.'

The former room-mate looked shocked and turned white.

Fardon tried to reassure him. 'Well don't worry, she would have got you by now if she was going to,' he said.

His friend smiled and recomposed himself, saying that he would like to introduce Fardon to his wife who had just entered the room. 'I think you may have met before,' he said.

Looking at the woman Fardon said that he did not recognize her and thought that a previous meeting was rather unlikely. Standing up to greet the woman his friend made the introduction. 'I'd like to introduce you to my wife Ann, and I think you ought to know ... her maiden name was Kerenov ... She got me after all!'

Fardon *didn't* recognize the woman. She was not the same figure who he had seen in the négligé, nor, it transpired, had Fardon's friend's wife had any psychic or ghostly experiences which could have shed light on the strange coincidence. The friends kept in touch and to this day have suffered no ill effects from the sexy ghost who used the same uncommon name. Nor have they solved the mystery of the poltergeist activity which occurred at the same time as Fardon's second sighting of the attractive ghost.

21   The Flagellated Nun

Watton Abbey in the East Riding of Yorkshire boasts a number of ghosts ranging from a dwarf gardener dressed in brown (who haunts the gardens) to cavaliers and various ghostly female figures, many of which appear to be covered in blood.

An ancient tale originally related by Alured the Abbot of Rievaulx Abbey tells of a four-year-old girl who in the 1100s was sent to Watton by the then Archbishop of York. His instructions were to have the girl brought up in holy orders as a pillar of the respectable church. Though the young girl was indeed trained as a nun, her inclinations were far from holy or respectable, and by the time she had become a young attractive woman, both her looks and her unbecoming behaviour caused much anxiety and resentment among her fellow sisters.

Monks from a nearby religious house visited Watton Abbey regularly, and before long it was rumoured that the young nun had taken one of the monks as her lover. Inevitably it was realized that she had become pregnant, and though the young monk escaped the consequences of his actions by leaving the holy orders, things were not to be so easy for the disgraced nun.

Following her enforced confession a meeting was called to discuss the appropriate punishment. Despite her obvious signs of pregnancy the nuns decided to strip the young woman naked, to stretch her on the floor for flagellation, and to scourge her naked body with rods. This unbelievably cruel torture was enforced with gusto in an orgy of flagellation which ripped the skin from her body and left her lying in a pool of her own blood. Almost at death's door, the nun was laid in a dungeon where she was given only bread and water, whilst the search began for the young monk who had earlier discharged himself from his holy orders. Having found her lover, the nuns carried out a brutal sexual assault on his private parts. So bad was the 'punishment' that the abbot who related the tale could not bring himself to fully describe what went on, only saying that he could not tell for 'fear of polluting the page'. Strangely, the following morning the nun was said to have been fully restored to her normal self, showing no signs of pregnancy, having had a healing dream in which a vision of the now dead Archbishop of York had appeared to her. She was now subjected to more flagellation and torture, eventually (it is said) dying from her injuries.

Since that time her bloody and naked ghost has been seen writhing in agony on a number of occasions. Many have described the figure as writhing in sexual ecstasy, while those who know of the tale associate the ghost's contortions with the pain of the punishment being endured. Sometimes an equally bloodied male figure has been seen under similar circumstances. Others tell of ghostly scenes of orgiastic nuns who frantically whip an unseen body on the ground, their faces reflecting released sexual frustrations and their obvious pleasure derived from the scourging of the poor young nun from the twelfth century.

22   The Gelded Ghost

Imagine the horror on a dark, stormy or foggy night, of coming across the ghost of a castrated man with bloody eye sockets, nailed to a door. Such is the grisly spectre that haunts Newcastle upon Tyne's quayside.

The ghost is reputedly to be seen haunting the alleyways near the old 'Cooperage' public house, which itself is said to be haunted by a number of ghosts including various phantom female figures and an Edwardian gentleman. A hooded monk is also said to frequent the place from time to time, whilst grunting, squealing and muttering voices drift through the air on moonless nights, when the whole quayside area can be transformed into an eerie almost film-set-like scene by the fog which grips the banks of the Tyne river.

The grisly castrated ghost has been seen on a number of occasions over the years since the sixteenth century, when it is said that a forerunner of the press gang was in the area, forcing able young men to enlist for passages on ships sailing to foreign parts.

Apparently a local barrel maker, Henry Hardwick, was among a band of around twenty Geordie youths who had been gathered together, and were being led towards a waiting ship on the quayside. Hardwick began to fight back, urging his fellow captives to fight for their lives. All was in vain however, as those involved in rounding up the reluctant sailors, were well armed ruffians who were used to the task, and would stop at nothing to deliver the men, and so earn their fee for each reluctant sailor supplied.

A fracas began in which the might and experience of the ruffians triumphed. Hardwick however was determined to escape, fighting in vain and shouting all the while for the others not to give up. At last the men had had enough of the trouble maker, and seizing on a hammer and some nails that were laid close by, they proceeded to nail Hardwick to the back door of the Cooperage where they proceeded to strip him of his clothes and beat him mercilessly. The terrorstruck captives were now forced to watch as an 'example' was made of the young barrel maker.

Taking a dagger from his side, one of the bloodthirsty sailors proceeded with great delight in gouging out the eyes of the crucified captive, finally severing his testicles in a sickening display of savage brutality.

Such is the story behind the appearance of the gelded ghost whose only crime in life was to resist being torn from the lifestyle he loved and who died in such horrible and intensely emotional circumstances, that the ghostly image of his eyeless and castrated bloodsoaked body appears to be locked in time, appearing and reappearing on moonless nights when the atmosphere and weather match those of the terrible night he died.

23   The Headless Sweetheart

The ghost of Ronald Travis' sweetheart was, until quite recent times, said to haunt an area where the old Midland Railways Brooke End signal box once stood. Her sighs, panting and orgasmic groans were reported on a number of occasions, despite the fact that the ghost appeared to have no head.

The story began in the early 1900s with the meeting of Ronald Travis, a young railway worker, and Marion Gorman, daughter of another railway employee. Travis had begun working at the Brooke End signal box, mainly on nights, and Marion Gorman had visited the box one evening looking for her father. From that point onwards an attraction quickly grew up between the two youngsters, who were both roughly the same age and from country family backgrounds.

At first Marion's parents approved of the relationship, but before long the young woman was abandoning her homely habits and spending more and more time with her young sweetheart. Her parents' resentment grew at her long periods of absence, particularly in the evenings when she would vanish for hours on end. Before long, her father decided to confront Travis in an effort to bring a bit of peace to the Gorman household. Travis however resented any interference from the girl's father, saying that the girl was old enough to make her own mind up as to whom she wanted to spend her time with.

It was one autumn evening when Mr Gorman remembered he had not posted the signal box duty roster for the next day, as was his normal practice. Dragging himself from his comfortable railwayman's cottage, he made the journey down to the signal box, only to find it apparently empty. Climbing the wooden stairs to the signal box door he gazed through the misty window expecting to find the signalman collapsed on the floor. What he did encounter however was the sight of his own daughter and Travis lying there in a state of semi-nakedness.

Though the girl was of age to take a lover, Gorman was extremely angry, more so perhaps because his daughter had deceived her parents, telling them that she would be elsewhere that evening. A tremendous row broke out between the three, ending in Marion being dragged away by her father who vowed he would never let the couple meet again.

From this point on, Marion became a virtual prisoner of her parents. Though they loved her dearly, a sense of overprotection ensured that Marion never left the house without one of her parents being with her. Before long however, the attraction between the two sweethearts prompted the young woman to plan a secret meeting, and one evening as her mother and father lay asleep in bed, she slipped from the cottage to meet secretly with Travis who was on nightshift at the signal box.

Marion crossed the line as the night train sped down the railway towards her, taking a risk in trying to beat it to the crossing point just down from the signal box. Though she had been spotted by the vigilant engine driver, and succeeded in crossing the line safely, her shoes slipped on a muddy patch on the steep embankment, and to the driver's horror, he saw the young girl fall beneath the locomotive's wheels.

The driver found a scene of horror. Not only was the young woman's mangled body covered in blood from top to bottom, but the train had run over her neck, completely severing her head.

Needless to say, Marion was killed outright and apart from the obvious distress and self-recrimination felt both by her loving parents and her adoring lover Ronald Travis, the story ended at the coroner's inquest where a verdict of accidental death was recorded. Travis and the parents all moved away in an attempt to escape from the terrible tragedy which had scarred their lives forever, but it seemed that Marion was not prepared to leave the area. From late in the 1940s a series of strange hauntings occurred.

A train guard named George Marsh was the first to spot the ghost of the girl. He was drinking a mug of tea while sitting on a goods train and waiting for a second locomotive to pass before a change of points would allow his own train to move on. As the train approached at speed, Marsh saw a young woman dressed in white dash across in front of it. Shouting out to her he was horrified to see the girl fall back under its wheels close to the signal box.

In view of others on the train who had heard his cry of alarm, Marsh rushed to the spot to find himself staring down at the decapitated body of a young woman in white. Frozen in horror, and shaking uncontrollably, he was shocked to see the figure disappear in front of his eyes.

Another incident was reported by Jan and Alice Marshall in the early 1950s, while picking blackberries in the same area. In the silence of the summer afternoon, only the twittering of the birds disturbed their pleasant occupation. As they approached the site of the old signal box they became aware of the obvious sound of a young woman in the act of making love with her partner, and thinking that they were about to disturb a young couple hidden in the undergrowth close by, they gave each other a knowing look and started moving in the opposite direction. This however, had no effect. The sound of the girl's mutterings and moanings seemed to follow them wherever they went. At last the Marshalls had had enough and Jan beckoned to his wife to cross the line to the other side. At the same moment the sound of a train could be heard approaching and Alice, without speaking, grabbed Jan's arm in an effort to hold him back from crossing the track until the train had passed. By now the moans and other noises had been muffled by the sound of the train which was almost upon them. Immediately and out of nowhere the couple noticed a young girl dressed in white, almost opposite them on the line, obviously intending to cross. Shouting out together in alarm the couple were relieved to see the long haired young girl dart across the track to the other side in the nick of time, and Jan gave a sigh of relief, shaking his head as he looked at his wife in disbelief.

As the train thundered past however, the couple saw that somehow the girl had not managed to make the safety of the other side of the rails. The bloody body of the girl lay upon the track, blood staining the ground and running in little rivulets between the sleepers. As his wife stood in horror with her hand to her mouth, Jan ran to the aid of the young woman. Bending down he was horrified to see that the train had completely severed her head, and blood stained her white dress from top to bottom. Instinctively he turned to his wife, telling her not to come, but to get help. However, no sooner had he spoken the words than the ghostly body evaporated into the air, leaving the distressed couple completely mystified.

Others too have heard the muffled moans and mutterings of love followed by the ghostly figure trying to beat a train at Brooke End. Remarkably, train drivers have never reported any incident at that spot since the terrible tragedy, though a number of people near the track have witnessed the ghostly re-run of Marion Gorman's last attempt to continue her love affair with her forbidden sweetheart. The ghostly figure and its sad (rather than frightening) sounds of love have not been seen or heard now for a number of years. Could it be that at last the ghost of Marion Gorman is resting in peace, and that in death Ronald Travis and Marion Gorman have found each other? It is a pleasant thought that the two sweethearts, whose life together was so tragically cut short, may at last have found peace together in another existence, beyond the realms of our earthly life.

24   The Groaning Bubbles

One of the strangest of hauntings is that of the groaning bubbles. Its 'home patch' is a small lake close to the village of Farlam, near Brampton in Cumbria. The haunting is said to have given its name to the lake known locally as 'Talkin Tarn'. A village nearby also carries the name of Talkin. Though why this should be so has never been explained. Could it be that 'Jessie', whose voice is said to emanate from the bubbles in Talkin Tarn, originally lived in that village?

Jessie certainly lived somewhere in the area in the mid 1800s and it is said that she would go down to the shores of the lake to make love to her boyfriend who unbeknown to Jessie was taking a different girl to the lakeside almost every evening in order to have his way with them. Before long Jessie was informed by a friend of 'something that she ought to know' – that the young man was making love to any woman he could get his hands on. Even worse was the fact that he was already engaged to the flaxen haired daughter of a rich local farmer. She too was oblivious to her fiancé's philandering ways.

Though shocked at the revelations, Jessie's evenings of passion meant too much to her, and she was not prepared to let her lover go. The story goes that whilst engaged in sex at the water's edge, Jessie told her lover that she was aware of his future engagement, but that if he went ahead with the wedding, she would inform the rich farmer and his daughter of all she knew. Though he protested his innocence, he knew he had been found out, and that his chance of marrying into a fortune was all but lost.

As the young couple lay in their naked embrace, a plan

grew in the young man's mind. Mounting the young girl once more, he engaged in passionate love-making so intense that his lover was completely oblivious to the water's lapping just beyond their heads at the edge of the lakeside. As her passion reached a climax her lover manoeuvred her body over the shallow edge of the lake until with a quick movement he pressed her head beneath the water. Ignoring her violent struggle for life, her lover used his superior strength to ensure she remained beneath the gentle waves until he was sure she was dead. It is said that her body was never found. Had it not been for a deathbed confession by her lover many years later when he was an old man, the mystery of Jessie's disappearance would never have been solved. He had evidently placed her body in a weighted sack and thrown her into the deepest part of the Tarn.

Jessie's ghost still haunts the spot where her murder took place. It begins by the sound of orgasmic moans and panting which stop abruptly. Then after a silent break lasting only seconds it comes – a series of bubbles breaking the surface at the water's edge and a slow pitiful moaning which also stops abruptly, just as it did the day that Jessie died in the throes of passion, at the hands of her unscrupulous lover.

25 The Urinating Goblin

A chance encounter whilst researching this book brought to light a rather strange story. The names of the people involved have been changed by request, though the place and incidents that occurred have been faithfully recorded.

It was in 1932 that Carl Brukker, a German writer, and his wife, were on holiday near Roscrea, an extremely picturesque area of Ireland. Brukker was compiling a book on religious and military remains and had taken off on his own one day to see one of the local round-towers for which Ireland is famous. It was a rainy day but despite the dismal weather Brukker had set off without any waterproof clothing and was already soaking wet when he came to the base of the tower.

Looking up at the 80 foot high structure, he forgot about his discomfort as the entrance to the tower caught his eye, for it was about 15 feet from the ground. The writer circled the building a number of times, taking photographs from various points of view before withdrawing to a distance in order to have his sandwiches and make a few scribbled notes.

As he wrote, he continued to look at the high entrance which fascinated him, when all of a sudden he caught sight of a movement at the entrance. As he was wearing glasses, his view was obscured somewhat, for the droplets of rain had gathered in small specks, blocking his vision. However, quickly wiping away the rain as best he could, he looked more intensely at the figure which by now appeared to be walking from the entrance to the ground at a steep angle without any visible means of support.

Brukker wrote:

I can remember thinking that perhaps he was a circus performer walking down a tightrope, though of course why this should be, I do not know, for there was not a circus anywhere near the place, and it was unlikely anyone would be practicing in such awful weather conditions.

The German visitor decided to take a closer look, but by the time he reached the base of the tower there was no one to be seen. Walking round the building from side to side, Brukker immediately became aware of what he presumed to be a small boy, dodging backwards and forwards, as if trying to hide on the opposite side of the building. As Brukker went right, the figure went left, and vice versa. Brukker again takes up the story:

> By now I was wet and bad tempered, and certainly not in the mood for playing games, so I began to walk away. As I got about ten feet from the base of the tower I became aware of someone small walking behind me and giggling stupidly. I continued to walk awhile, pretending not to notice him and then suddenly I stopped and turned round on my heels.

Brukker was not prepared for what he saw. Trailing behind him was a tiny figure of a man about 3 feet tall, naked except for a brown floppy top hat.

'I can only describe him as a goblin,' said Brukker, who recorded the fact that the sheer ugliness of the man's features made him sick, for he was covered in warts, had a large misshapen nose, and worst of all had a large disproportionately thick phallus which hung almost to the ground.

Brukker continued:

> The goblin seemed fully aware that I was unable to take my eyes off his giant member, and giggling like a maniac, he began to swing it round and round like an enormous piece of rope. At this point I was walking backwards and stumbled over a rock, the hair on the back of my neck standing on end. As I did so the ugly misshapen goblin rushed towards me. In fear of danger I held my hands to my face expecting a blow when I suddenly experienced

something hot and wet hitting me. The goblin was urinating on me. As I looked up more now in anger than horror, the ugly being began to fade away slowly, taking on the appearance of the ghosts you see in the pictures. With a strange dance he began to laugh loudly. Before I knew it he had faded to a point where he looked nothing more than a featureless grey shadow, and began to drift across the ground back towards the tower.

Why I did it I don't know, but my first reaction was to lift up my arm to my nose and smell it, presumably because of the urine shower which I had just experienced. Strangely not only did my clothes not smell, but I realised that my previously wet clothing was now completely dry. Even the spots of rain on my glasses had disappeared, and through the clear lenses I could just see the gnomelike figure, once more returning through the air to the door of the tower in the same way that he had come down.

Brukker goes on to state that almost immediately his clothes gradually became wet once more 'in exactly the way you would expect dry clothes to do if you had just gone out in the rain'.

Brukker immediately went home. He did not tell his wife of his experience, though he did bring her to the spot the very next day in the hope that she might by sheer chance confirm another sighting of the ugly goblin-like ghost. Nothing untoward occurred. The writer admits that he was a believer in ghosts, though at the time of the incident, nothing was further from his mind, nor had he ever experienced any unusual happenings before this time (or indeed expected to).

His wife was aware of his beliefs but was said to be much more sceptical, and Brukker says that he never did reveal the incident to her (she died in 1940) 'for fear of being laughed out of the house'. As a writer he was used to researching stories thoroughly, and over the next two or three years he attempted to find some explanation for what had happened. No similar ghostly happenings had been reported locally (though some suggested it might have been one of 'the little people' that he had come across). Brukker even visited a psychiatrist in a bid to see if he may have imagined the whole thing. However, under hypnosis he recalled the incident exactly as it had occurred on the day, and satisfied that his own sanity was not in question. Brukker let the incident drop. He began some time later writing down his experiences with the intention of publishing an article on the subject. However, a stroke soon after left him severely paralysed and his notes were passed on to a close friend who belonged to a small local group which studied paranormal happenings. This man later died and the group (of which he was secretary) disbanded. His widow sadly destroyed the many files of ghost stories which had been collected over the years though being Irish she had kept this particular story out of personal interest.

Thanks to a chance encounter the incident has been brought to light after almost thirty years and is now for the first time revealed to the general public.

26   Ravished by a Glass Tube in the Tower of London

The Tower of London is renowned for its many ghosts. Knights in armour, headless figures, and countless dead prisoners including the famous Anne Boleyn.

This tale, however, is quite different from any other, for the ghost appeared as a kind of swirling glass-like tube. Even more strange is that the story dates from 1817, and was originally related by Mr Swifte, keeper of the crown jewels.

One version of the story repeated in *Haunted Homes & Family Legends* gives part of Swifte's account:

In 1814 I was appointed Keeper of the Crown Jewels in the Tower, where I resided with my family till my retirement in 1852. One Saturday night in October 1817, about 'the witching hour', I was at supper with my wife, her sister, and our little boy, in the living-room of the Jewel House, which then comparatively modernised is said to have been the 'doleful prison' of Anne Boleyn, and of the ten bishops whom Oliver Cromwell piously accommodated therein...

Swifte goes on to describe the room as being irregularly shaped with three doors and two 9 foot × 2 foot windows, having between them a stone chimney which projected into the room, and upon which was a large oil painting. He tells that on the night in question both windows were covered by heavy cloth curtains and the doors were closed. Two candles provided the only light.

> I sate [*sic*] at the foot of the table, my son on my right hand, his mother fronting the chimney piece, and her sister on the opposite side. I had offered a glass of wine and water to my wife, when on putting it to her lips, she paused, and exclaimed, 'Good God! what is that?' I looked up, and saw a cylindrical figure like a glass tube, seemingly about the thickness of my arm, and hovering between the ceiling and the table; its contents appeared to be a dense fluid, white and pale azure, like to the gathering of a summer-cloud, and incessantly mingling within the cylinder. This lasted about two minutes, when it began slowly to move before my sister-in-law; then, following the oblong shape of the table, before my son and myself; passing behind my wife, it paused for a moment over her right shoulder [observe, there was no mirror opposite to her in which she could behold it]. Instantly she crouched down, and with both hands covering her shoulder, she shrieked out, 'O Christ! it has seized me!'

Swifte goes on to tell of striking out at the strange ghostly figure, which was seen only by himself and his wife, and that neither his son nor his sister-in-law observed the figure. The servants were called to attend to Mrs Swifte, who later suffered no ill effects from the visitation.

There are many and varied accounts of this particular haunting, and they have been added to and altered over the years. Though Swifte's own version should be the most authentic, it would seem that his account omitted details, in order to protect his wife's modesty.

Another version of the tale, given by one of the servants involved, was repeated in another nineteenth century book, *Fantasms of Old London*. It closely follows that related by Swifte himself, but it does enlarge upon the story and gives a fascinating insight into the events of that night.

> … we arrived in the room to find Mr Swifte in much agitation, ushering his son and his sister-in-law out of the room, telling them to wait in the children's room upstairs. Mrs Swifte lay upon the floor, her whole bodice agape and her breast bare, showing red risen teeth marks upon them, which were repeated upon her shoulders and neck. She was thrashing around as if engaged in close relations with a lover, but these movements quickly subsided upon our

arrival. Shortly she came fully round, adjusted her clothing and calmly began to tell us what she had perceived in the moments before.

It would seem that a kind of spirit or ghost had come upon her in the shape of a glass roll which swirled within with strange gasses or clouds. Though she could not see him, nor hear him, she perceived in her mind, non the less, a bluff, hearty man, behind her who told her he must have her body, despite the company of her family. Within seconds he had seized her shoulder and pulled open her bodice, all the while biting passionately at her skin. Though Madam went on to tell us in immodest fashion of all that took place, she begged that nothing should be repeated to others for fear her husband's and her own honour be at stake. I can only now tell you this which is common knowledge, but can repeat no more of the events of that night, save that Mrs Swifte appeared to be completely normal and suffered no ill effects or further visits from the wild spirit.

What is one to make of such a strange story? Twentieth century 'sci-fi' imagery in the nineteenth century? A sexual attack by an unknown entity before husband and family? A ghost whose physical body and voice cannot be seen or heard, yet can be visualized and experienced via the mind?

It is difficult to imagine an elaborate hoax which involved a woman deliberately acting in such a way before her own son and sister, yet the question remains: Why were only Mr and Mrs Swifte aware of the ghost, whilst the sister-in-law and son were not? Why, one must ask, should Mrs Swifte go into minute detail when relating her experience to the servants? Was this pre-planned for a purpose, or was Mrs Swifte simply being genuine and honest towards her trusted maids? (One at least does seem to have revealed only what she thought was common knowledge.)

If it had been a hoax, surely a more conventional type of ghost, perhaps a cavalier or a headless figure, would have been more believable to a nineteenth century maid than a floating glass tube filled with vapour? What is more, both Swifte and his wife were well-respected people in a responsible position, and unlikely to want to jeopardize their standing, let alone risk losing Mr Swifte's well-paid position at the tower.

All in all, the mystery remains unsolved. In the light of the evidence presented to us, we must accept that a very unusual type of haunting did actually take place. A haunting that is perhaps unique not only in the records of ghostly happenings in the tower, but also amongst the thousands of strange and ghostly tales that have been told through the centuries. It remains as mystifying now as it must have been to the nineteenth century keeper of the crown jewels – A glass tube ghost coming to ravish your wife on a cold Saturday night is certainly no ordinary occurrence.

27 The Skulls That Had Sex

In an area between Bolton and Bury in Lancashire lies land which has now long been a built-up area, but was once rolling farmlands. Located in this rural setting was Timberbottom Farm, an agricultural homestead of little note, except that within its walls two skulls were kept.

The human skulls, one male and one female, were originally found together in the farmer's ditch, where a small trickling stream flowed through. How long the skulls had been interred in their watery grave was not known, though it was strange that no other human bones were found, despite an intensive search.

Country superstitions die hard in rural areas, and it was decided that the skulls would be put inside the building in order to act as a talismanic protection against evil forces. The pair were scrubbed clean, oiled and placed in a prominent place upon the mantelshelf above the fireplace in one of the upstairs bedrooms. Peace did indeed reign at the farmhouse for a number of years.

However, whilst cleaning the room, sometime around 1835, the lady of the house accidentally dropped one of the skulls onto the floor, chipping a large piece of bone from the base. This in itself caused no ill effect until a few days later when the son of the household took the damaged bones away for repair. From then on a whole series of poltergeist activities began to occur.

That very evening, a male voice was heard coming from the bedroom in which the now solitary skull was kept. Its words were indistinct but the man was obviously distressed, almost as if shouting for someone lost in the dark. The farmer and his son rushed to the room expecting to find intruders and wondering just what was going on. As they opened the bedroom door they found it bathed in an eerie light. Objects were seen to be mysteriously floating round in mid-air, as if being moved from place to place by some unseen hand.

Country people of that time were much more at home with supernatural explanations. It was decided that the separation of the skulls had caused this unwanted activity, and next day, without delay, the female skull was quickly repaired and replaced in its usual place.

One might expect this action to have settled matters down, but it was not to be so. It would seem that once the door to the 'other world' had been opened, the spirits of the skulls had chosen to remain on the earthly plain. Two nights later, whilst eating their evening meal after a long hard day on the land, the family heard a bump upstairs. This was followed by more strange noises including the voices of two different men and a woman, all shouting and screaming as if involved in some great argument. As the clamour became louder, bangs, crashes and weeping sounds came from the upstairs room, and despite their obvious fear the men quietly climbed the wooden stairs to peer through the gap under the bedroom door.

What the father and son saw filled them with terror, for the bedroom seemed to be lit once more by a strange green light. Two ghostly male figures could be seen dressed in medieval costume, pushing and shoving each other round the room, knocking over objects which instead of falling to the floor, simply ricocheted off the walls, only to swirl round the room slowly like some orbiting planet. The men were evidently in violent disagreement, though the language they spoke was either not English, or of some strange dialect which could not be deciphered by the watching pair.

As the men stared open-mouthed at this strange vision, a wispy figure of a woman in a long red dress appeared to try and separate the fighting men. She was pushed to the ground violently in the struggle, and on hitting the floor disappeared into thin air. Her disappearance was quickly followed by that of the two medieval gentlemen, and within a short time, the floating objects returned to their normal places and the ghostly light which had filled the room faded.

A number of ideas were tried to quieten the restless skulls, including sprinkling them with holy water, burying them in the local churchyard, and returning them to the ditch where they were discovered. None of these worked, and the hauntings continued in the room as before, with bangings, shouting, weeping and other unnerving activity. Finally, the skulls were brought back to the house and placed upon the large family Bible. For many months all was quiet and at last the family decided to try placing the skulls as they once had been, together on the mantelpiece, and the Bible was put in the living-room cupboard.

That evening a strange mewing sound came from the bedroom, and with heavy hearts, the family feared that the poltergeist activity was to begin once more. Male moans also began to come from the room, growing louder and faster and interspersed with heavy breathing. Before long it was realized that what the family was hearing was the sound of a couple engaged in the sexual act.

Creeping upstairs, the men once more looked under the door. This time the room was in complete darkness, but the noises were distinctly heard to emanate from the direction of the skulls. There was no other explanation in the farmer's minds – the spirits of the dead couple were making love.

Strangely, from this point onwards, the house remained quiet apart from the sporadic sounds of lovemaking, and there was no more shouting, knocking or weeping. Neither were the three ghostly figures ever seen again in the farmhouse.

Country gossip revealed a number of explanations for the happenings at Timberbottom, the most likely being the story of a young farmer who fell in love with a daughter of the Bradshaw family of nearby Bradshaw Hall. It is said that the affair was not condoned by the Bradshaw family. Engaged in an argument with the girl's brother, the young man was accidentally slain by a blow across the head. It is said that the girl died shortly afterwards of grief and despair, and that out of respect for their daughter, the repenting Bradshaws ensured that the two lovers were buried together.

Though the story appears to tie up neatly with the events at the old farmstead, two striking questions remain. How did the two skulls (separated from the rest of their skeletons) come to be found in the tiny streamlet which ran through the ditch at the edge of the field near Timberbottom Farm, and more to the point, where are they now?

Bradshaw Hall itself has now been demolished, though a single skull which once rested on a Bible in the study is now to be seen at Turton Tower. Could this third skull have a connection with the story? Could it be the other male ghost figure who was seen in the bedroom at Timberbottom? Or is it actually one of the two skulls which stood for many years on the mantelshelf, its aged bony jaws uttering the sounds of love? If this is so and the skulls have once more been separated, who knows what strange poltergeist activity may yet take place before the skulls are brought together again? Let's hope for everyone's sake that if and when this does occur, the skulls can be physically fixed together by some means. In this way, the lovers who have so many times been separated from each other after death, may at last be joined together in a gesture from the world of the living to the world of the dead.

28   Fanny of Cock Lane

Many of London's ancient dwellings claim to hold the title of the capital's most famous haunted house. This was the case with 20, Cock Lane, which was demolished in 1979.

The building was believed to have been built not long after the Great Fire of London in 1666 and always suffered from poltergeist activity for as long as anyone could remember. Moving furniture, scratching noises, tappings at the window and various bumps in the night became commonplace, and it is said that one of the buildings' tenants, John Kent, would delight in unnerving his servants with ghostly tales of what had gone on in the house.

Around the late 1750s, Kent employed a young house-servant named Fanny, whose surname is not recorded. She was reputedly a simple superstitious country girl who Kent found could be easily manipulated. She was extremely frightened of the noises and other phenomena caused by the resident poltergeist, and before long her employer had convinced her that he was able to communicate with the ghosts of the house. They could only be calmed, he claimed, by sexual activity taking place within the walls of the building.

Fanny was led to believe that Kent's wife was denying him his conjugal rights and it was this that was bringing about the paranormal activity. The naïve young girl was persuaded to engage in sexual activity with her employer and before long a passionate affair ensued.

Time passed and Fanny became bored with the relationship. However, the noises had strangely failed to manifest themselves during the time she was having a

sexual relationship with Kent, and she continued to believe (rightly or wrongly) that this was due to her love affair. Though she continued to join her employer in his bedroom, Fanny now found more and more excuses not to, and within a short time Kent began to realize that his power over the servant girl was not as strong as it had been.

Once more he warned Fanny that the ghosts had communicated with him, telling him that they were becoming uneasy at the lack of sexual activity and that if it did not increase, the knockings, bangings and tappings could recommence. Furthermore, he warned, should this happen, then whoever was responsible would die shortly afterwards. Making it quite plain to the servant girl that it was not he who was responsible for the lack of sexual activity in the house but her, he insisted that to save her life she should immediately resume their sexual relations at a more frequent rate.

Fanny was evidently not convinced by her employer's story for she continued to visit him less and less in his bedchamber. It was only when the rappings and bumps began to occur once more that she became frightened, remembering what Kent had told her. Confiding in a friend, she was advised to ignore the poltergeist activity (which, she was told, was probably the work of Kent himself) and to end her affair with him.

But Fanny found her master would not easily accept the fact that their relationship was over. He continued to pass on death threats which he claimed had been made by the 'spirits of the house' and only agreed to an end to the relationship when Fanny threatened to tell his wife about everything that had gone on. Kent was furious.

'Be it as you wish,' he told her, 'but mark my words young woman, you will be dead within the month.'

Strange as it may seem, Fanny died shortly afterwards. Rumours spread that Kent had been having an affair with the servant girl and had poisoned her with arsenic in order to stop the details of their affair becoming public. The poltergeist activity continued, growing more and more in intensity until finally Kent could stand it no longer and moved home. The ghostly activity neither followed Kent nor ceased for the new owner of the house. Its new tenant, an Elizabeth Parsons, began to suffer the disturbances almost from the day she moved in.

Parsons also revelled in widely publicising the activities of the resident poltergeists, and before long the ghosts of Cock Lane had become well known throughout the city. The writer Samuel Johnson was among the many investigators who visited the house. Thomas Carlyle, the writer, in *The Illusion of Time* states:

> Again, could anything be more miraculous than an actual authentic Ghost? The English Johnson longed, all his life to see one; but could not, though he went to Cock Lane, and thence to the church vaults, and tapped on coffins...

Johnson did indeed become sceptical of Elizabeth Parsons' claims and declared her a fraudster, a claim that was taken up by the authorities who took great pains to discover whether Elizabeth or her family could be the cause of the knockings and other activities. The investigation was long and thorough, even going to such extremes as binding the family's arms and legs and suspending furniture on ropes above the floor in order to see if the noises still occurred. Unfortunately for the Parsons, the house was completely peaceful during the period when they were tied up, and the family were jailed for fraud, though they continued to insist that they had taken no part in causing the strange noises.

Many years later it is said that similar strange tappings were found to be coming from Fanny's grave, although this was denied by the authorities. However, to quieten persistent rumours, an exorcism was performed and consequently the coffin was reinterred in the crypt of St John's Church, Clerkenwell.

Curious ghost hunters who were examining the case in the mid 1800s are said to have located the coffin and opened it up. Inside was the perfectly preserved body of Fanny of Cock Lane, her features as beautiful as the day she died. Some say her preservation was a sign that her ghost had never left her body (accounting for the strange knockings which were said to emanate from inside). More sceptical observers argued that there was a scientific explanation for the preservation of Fanny's body. In the dawn of forensic science in the 1800s, it had been noted that the bodies of those who died of arsenic poisoning tended not to rot in the same way as ordinary bodies did. Arsenic effectively preserved the corpse in a state of mummification.

Could it be then, that despite the obvious evidence of poltergeist activity, there was a more sinister earthly reason for the death of Fanny of Cock Lane? Could the woman have been poisoned by her former employee, as had been rumoured well over a century before?

29   The Marriage-bed Monk

The Augustan house of Newstead Priory in Notting-
hamshire has been the home of a number of Lord Byrons,
including the famed poet, who put pen to paper in order
to record the building's malicious monk – said to haunt
residents of the priory upon their deathbeds. The eerie
black figure was also noted for its visits to newly married
couples engaged in the passion of their first night together
in the building.

> By the marriage-bed of their lords 'tis said
> He flits on the bridal eve;
> And 'tis held as faith, to their bed of death
> he comes (but not to grieve).
>
> from 'Don Juan' by Lord Byron

Byron inherited the building when still a boy, and it is
said he spent a very happy childhood there, revelling in
the stories of terrible deeds which were supposed to have
taken place during the 400 years when the Black Augustan
monks roamed the building. It is said that when King
Henry VIII confiscated the building and its lands, a
number of the monks who were secretly members of a
'magical inner brotherhood' placed a curse upon those
who were to take over the abbey lands.

It is certainly known that a cowled figure has appeared
at a number of christenings, his dark and dismal face
scowling at the start of yet another generation of
unwanted residents. Likewise, whenever a death took
place, the evil hooded monk was to be seen gloating at the
bedside of the unattended corpse when anyone entered
the room. Weddings too did not escape a visit from the

malicious monk – Byron himself was said to have seen the ghost at his own marriage ceremony, although he described this monk as 'smiling and cheerful'.

Newlywed couples, in the bliss of their first sexual embrace, were said to be particular targets. Following such a marital coupling, a young man reputedly found himself streaming with blood from his sexual organs. Rushing to examine the horrific feeling of hot sticky blood running down his legs, he was amazed to find no trace of it whatsoever, but in the flickering light of the candle he saw the scowling figure of the monk looking over him. It gave a wicked wry smile and slowly disappeared. On another occasion a newlywed man and wife were said to have found themselves locked together and unable to part ' … as if bound by unseen tethers', and they too saw the evil black figure looming over them. They remained in this stage until their cries caught the attention of a servant, whose presence seemed to 'break the spell' and the couple found themselves able to move as normal as the monk vanished.

Only once was a band of monks seen, and on this occasion the evil figure himself seemed to act as though he was being haunted. As a young man and woman undressed on the second night of their marriage, the malicious monk appeared in the corner of the bedroom, a sickly smell became apparent and strange pools of a white, sticky substance began to bubble on the floor. Frozen with fear, the couple had no time to panic before the next strange thing happened. Out of the wall at the other end of the bedchamber came the figure of another monk. He was dressed in the same way as the black monk but was not wearing a hood and was carrying a cross, as if leading a procession. He was followed by another, then another, and yet another, until a stream of 'a half score' had begun to cross the room, two abreast. Though the parade of monks did not communicate with the black monk in any way (indeed, they did not appear to even know of his presence), he was obviously extremely perturbed by their appearance. Immediately the bubbling mess on the floor evaporated and the evil figure himself vanished, though not without great difficulty. His agitated mannerisms seemed to indicate that he was having problems in leaving the site of the haunting.

Though the incident did nothing to curb further hauntings by the cowled figure, it would seem that he himself had had a terrifying experience. Could it be that this is the only known case of a ghost in the act of haunting, being scared 'to death' by other ghosts haunting *him* ...?

30   The Naked Five
Who Refused to Die

Margaret Denning's experience with ghosts was most unusual. It took place in Trafalgar Square, London, early one morning in December 1990. Margaret had been to an all-night party and had been given a lift to Trafalgar Square where her boyfriend had agreed to pick her up. To her dismay she found herself alone in the square, the streets eerily quiet and the air cold and crisp. As she nervously looked around for any sign of her boyfriend, she was startled to see a group of five naked men coming towards her in the distance. The men were whooping with joy and obviously not feeling the effects of cold. Spotting a girl standing alone, the men moved towards Margaret, who instinctively opened her handbag and took out a sharp-ended comb in order to defend herself.

The men gathered round Margaret, still whooping, and cavorted round and round in a circle, in what Margaret assumed was a drunken dance. Obviously aware that their nakedness was offending her, two of the group taunted her with their genitals, bowing their bodies inwards as they danced. Still thinking that the group were a bunch of drunken yobbos rather than anyone who meant to do her real harm, the frightened young woman showed great sense of composure by simply standing still and threatening that she would 'stick you where it hurts' if they did not leave her, adding that her boyfriend would be there any minute.

The threats had no effect, and so in desperation the young woman took her comb and attempted to stab at the genitals of the two who were continuing to press their bodies in her direction as they danced.

Almost at once a voice called her name from somewhere in the distance. It was Margaret's boyfriend, who was now running towards her with a slightly amused look on his face. The hair on Margaret's neck stood on end for, as she looked, the five dancing naked men slowly vanished into thin air in front of her eyes. By the time her boyfriend had asked her what she had been doing running around in circles waving a comb, all she could do was burst into tears in his arms.

It took some time before Margaret convinced her boyfriend of what had actually happened that night, for he just assumed she had been drinking heavily and was indulging in some drunken dance in order to stave off boredom and the cold of the morning. Though a non-believer in ghosts, he related the story to some of his friends who published it in a student magazine.

No explanation was ever given for the strange haunting, but it may be that events which took place close by in the fifteenth century might have some bearing on the matter.

In those days the death sentence could be given for relatively minor offences, and London's most famous gallows was situated at Tyburn, now the site of Marble Arch. It is not surprising that such a site should be known for its hauntings, and there were said to be untold numbers of different ghosts and spectres wandering about, particularly at night when the streets were largely unlit.

In 1447 crowds gathered for another public hanging. The criminals in this case were five members of an alleged gang of ruffians, who had conspired together to commit murder. The group of men had protested their innocence, new evidence had been uncovered at the last minute, and a possible reprieve was being spoken of, but the waiting crowds were becoming impatient. Chanting broke out and in order to quieten them, the attending minister clambered up onto the platform where the five nooses hung. The clergyman stated that the 'ceremony' would be delayed for another five minutes as it was believed a reprieve was on the way, and that he was sure the God-fearing citizens would not wish to see innocent men die.

On the contrary, the crowd were not interested in whether the men were innocent or guilty. Their entertainment was being spoilt, and amidst a clamour of boos, hisses, catcalls, and thrown missiles, the minister hurriedly left the gallows, shaking his head at the hangman and indicating that the prisoners should be brought out.

The hanging took place immediately, much to the glee of the rabble, and in line with the custom of the time, the dead bodies were taken down, stripped, and their clothes thrown to the crowds. Next came the drawing and quartering of the bodies, but before this could be done, a horseman galloped up to the gallows carrying the reprieve which acknowledged the innocence of the five men and would have set them free.

It is said that as the reprieve was read out to the crowd by the angry minister, who stated that they should all ask God's forgiveness for the unjust killings which had just taken place, something extremely strange took place.

From each of the bodies lying naked on the ground emerged a misty naked ghost which gradually formed into a solid body, indistinguishable from those lying upon the ground. The crowd of hundreds fell silent at this strange sight, so much so that even those at the back were able to clearly hear the ghosts rejoice at their reprieve and ask the hangman for their clothes back.

It is said that the hangman, though taken aback by the strange event, composed himself enough to ask the crowd to throw back the clothes, but received no positive response from the assembled throng.

In disgust, the naked five stormed down the steps of the gallows, some weeping with joy, some silent, and others laughing at their supposed escape from death. Still in total silence, it is said that the stunned crowd watched as the solid-looking ghostly figures walked through them and vanished into the distance down Oxford Street.

A group of five naked male ghosts were seen at various

periods over the next 200 years, running in apparent joy through the streets of London, around the site of Tyburn, but no reports have been made of such a haunting since the mid 1700s. None that is, until that winter's morning in 1990. Could it be that the experience of Margaret Denning in Trafalgar Square heralds the return of these five naked, innocent men, who refused to die on the gallows of Tyburn almost 500 years earlier?

31 The Gypsy Girl
and her Lesbian Lover

It is said that in the 1600s a band of gypsies regularly camped on open land just outside Staxton, a small village near Scarborough, Yorkshire, and that a romance grew between a young gypsy girl and the daughter of a local innkeeper-cum-farmer who she would call on when in the area. Though the stated purpose of her visit was said to be in order to 'charm the cattle' into producing more milk, it was not long before the young girls were discovered locked in a naked embrace together in one of the haylofts nearby. The 'unnatural coupling' was blamed on witchcraft and instances of 'charming' being practised by the gypsy girl, but because a number of locals were aware of the sexual leanings of the innkeeper's daughter, it was felt best to let the matter rest. The girls were kept separate from that point onwards.

Approximately five years later the gypsies were once again encamped near the village. They had arrived to make preparations for attending the Scarborough Fair. One evening the gypsy girl (now a young woman) vanished whilst out picking fungi to sell the next morning. Rumours quickly spread that she had been murdered by the innkeeper, who since the incident with his daughter had held a grudge against all gypsies and travellers, allowing none of them to enter his premises. Though a search was made of the fields and woodlands around Staxton, her body was never found, and some began to suspect that the innkeeper had burnt her body during a tree-clearing operation which had taken place at about the time the young woman vanished.

A number of sightings were reported over the next three or four years of a naked young woman's ghost, which was said to emerge through the wall of the inn around the time of Scarborough Fair. The ghost was said to walk across the field behind the inn, and vanish through the wall into the hayloft where the two young women had been found in a naked sexual embrace all those years ago. These hauntings reputedly stopped when the innkeeper's daughter died of a fever. It was believed locally that the innkeeper had buried the bones of the gypsy girl in his cellar and that her ghost was forever looking for the companionship of her female lover. Why else? they argued, had the hauntings stopped when the innkeeper's daughter had died. Surely, they said, this was because the girls were now united in death.

Another version of the tale states that although the sexual relationship between the two girls did happen, the meetings were actually condoned by their fathers, who were said to be involved in illicit deals involving unnatural practices. In this second version of the tale, strange black magic ceremonies are said to have taken place in the cellar, where animals were sacrificed whilst the two young girls cavorted naked together. The 'magic bones' were then exchanged for gold by the gypsy who would sell them to local wisemen and witches. The story of the gypsy girl's death and her ghostly haunting was said to have been concocted in order to keep away locals when the illegal deals and ceremonies were taking place.

Though the story is no doubt based on truth, the actual inn was never identified by name. No one could prove that the gypsy girl was murdered and it could be that she simply decided to run off. What is strange however, is that in 1989, a number of bones were found in the cellar of an old country inn in Staxton. Could these have included the bones of the long-lost gypsy girl, or if not, were they the uncollected remains of sacrificed animals from one of the inn's magical ceremonies?

It was also in 1989 when a story appeared in the local Scarborough paper. Tony Nacey, the owner of the

Gantondale Inn at Staxton, discovered a pile of old mixed bones in the north wall of the building whilst converting a cellar to a sauna. The ancient walls of the cellar, which had been sealed for centuries, were said to be three feet thick and made of chalkstone. The history of the Gantondale Inn reveals that it formerly served as a staging post for the Whitby to Beverley stagecoach and was originally known by its original name 'The New Inn'. Of course, whether this was in fact the same inn mentioned in the story of the young gypsy girl is not known, but the coincidences suggest that it may have been. This particular hostelry was certainly said to be haunted by a grey lady who arrived by a ghost stagecoach and walked through the building wall, finally vanishing in the present dining-room. In addition, the building was reputedly the scene of a murder over a bag of gold which is still said to lie hidden on the premises (another fascinating similarity to the tales told of the strange events of the 1600s).

In 1985 the old inn was gutted by fire and whilst flames raged through the building, a face peered out through the smoke at an upstairs window. Speeding quickly to the rescue, a fireman climbed a ladder only to find an empty room.

The finding of the bones in the cellar wall was not itself without incident. Mr Nacey described how they were discovered during the drilling of a hole which was to take the newly-installed water pipes. As the drill broke through, a distinct change in temperature was felt by all in the room. The landlord estimated that the temperature fell by almost 20 degrees, saying, 'It became so cold that when someone breathed out, you could see your own breath'. As previously stated, the cellar had been blocked up for centuries for no apparent reason. Mr Nacey told how the workmen refused to return to their work until he had gathered together all of the bones. The cardboard box he put them in remained very cold to the touch for a long time afterwards and the experience proved so unnerving to those involved that none wanted to go to bed that evening, though nothing untoward did in fact occur. The bones, which were of mixed animal origin, were of considerable age and were described at the time as 'very yellow and dry'.

Mr Nacey was evidently unaware of the tale of the lesbian gypsy girl and the innkeeper's daughter, nor had he heard stories of former hauntings at a local inn by her naked ghost. He stated simply and honestly in his own words that, 'No explanation can be found so far to account for the presence of the bones at the Inn'.

32   The Ghosts Who Broke Wind

It would seem that in the eighteenth and early nineteenth centuries, St James' Street, London, was a street containing many a haunted building.

A short account in a magazine of the mid 1800s recalls the unusual tale of one particular house which no one would inhabit because of the obnoxious sounds and smells which closely resembled that of people violently breaking wind.

Early tenants in the building would wake at night to find themselves surrounded by an odour which was variously described as 'rotten eggs', 'rotting cabbage', or 'sulphurous fumes'. At first bad drainage was suspected, but repeated investigations failed to find the cause. The nuisance went from bad to worse, until eventually the owners vacated the building and let the rooms instead. This was no solution however, for within a very short time tales began to circulate, and before long even itinerant travellers became aware of its reputation for bad smells and would not stay in the building.

The sounds of breaking wind were first reported around 1750, when a new owner took over the building. After buying the place, a fair amount of restoration work was undertaken. The ancient wooden panelling was temporarily removed and the walls beneath were treated with quick lime (evidently in an attempt to cure the problem of foul smells). This only seemed to make matters worse, for when the panels were put back in place, sightings of strange transparent unclothed figures apparently drifted in and out of the rooms at night, laughing silently to themselves as they seemed to compete with each other as to who could break wind the loudest.

For a short time the 'blashing ghosts', as they became known, were an attraction, even drawing guests who were actually willing to pay to stay overnight in the rooms. However, within a short time the novelty value ceased and the new owner, unwilling to occupy the building himself, could not find anyone who would stay as a paying tenant.

Other owners took over the building, all evidently unaware of its ghostly reputation. Naturally, as soon as they were aware of the strange happenings, they all tried to find some other unsuspecting stranger who was willing to take the place off their hands at a knock-down price.

The building stood empty for many years, until a young man, recently returned from abroad, decided to take up lodgings there. After only one night in the building he refused to stay any longer, complaining of the terrible noises and smells, and the attentions of ghostly figures which constantly drew apart the curtains at the bottom of his four-poster bed and peered at him, obviously to judge the effect the wind-breaking was having upon the unfortunate occupier.

Another long period occurred without tenants, until eventually it was decided that the old interior panelling should be completely removed and the building should be refurbished. The ancient wooden fabric was burned on a makeshift bonfire and from this time onwards the noises and smells were said to disappear, though strangely, a new, less offensive haunting was said to take its place. On still dark nights when the moon was full, the sound of ghostly footsteps could be heard from time to time, following inhabitants around the house from room to room – and occasionally, just occasionally, a sweeter smell wafted round the draughty corridors. The scent of roses had replaced the acrid fumes of the years before.

33   The Wanton Witch
of the Scottish Glen

Robin Green was a casualty of the Second World War. During an enemy attack on his unit, he was so seriously wounded that doctors were unable to save his injured arm, which consequently had to be amputated. Because of this disability Green never worked after the war ended, and instead spent his time in outdoor pursuits, often going off on camping trips with his wife and child. Following the death of his wife in 1953 he became a keen lone camper and travelled many miles each year, taking a delight in visiting a new part of the country with every trip.

On one of these trips in 1955, he was visiting the Inverness area, and had set up camp in an isolated valley. Though he rarely spent more than one night at any location, Green was suffering from an attack of sickness and stomach ache, and armed with a prescription from a local doctor, he decided to stay a number of nights in order to rest until he felt better.

On the first night of his stay he was disturbed from his slumbers by the sound of the tent flaps being opened. Looking up, he was amazed to see the figure of a wizened old lady staring at him through the opening. She did not attempt to enter the tent, but simply beckoned Green towards her, whilst repeatedly inviting him to make love to her in the most graphic and filthy language imaginable. Green later remarked that he had not been frightened by the experience, thinking that perhaps this was some drunken old lady who lived in a croft nearby. His

response was to tell her politely to go back home and leave him alone.

On the following two nights the experience was repeated, and having had enough, Green decided that if it should happen again, he would get her name and report her to the local police the next morning.

As was expected, the fourth night brought a repeat of the events and Robin Green put his plan into action. Following her tirade of obscene invitations, he pretended to show interest in her sexual suggestions and tried to carry out a conversation with her as she remained in the same position, with her head in the doorway and her body outside. On being asked her name she reacted violently, shouting hysterically and repeatedly that she was Isobel Gowdie of Auldearne, a place name which meant nothing to Green then.

After being threatened with the police, the old hag rushed outside and began shaking the tent violently. Green followed her out in anger, only to find the old woman gone but the tent still shaking violently on its own. It was at this point that the lone camper realized just how strange these events were, and became suddenly frightened. He immediately vacated his tent in fear and did not return until the following day.

In the morning Green remembered the name of the old woman and the town which she claimed to have come from, and wrote them down in his notebook before leaving Scotland for good, vowing never to go camping again.

Yet for reasons known only to himself, the haunted camper never did report the incident to the police. Perhaps he thought that he had been hallucinating, from the strong medication he was taking, or that his story would be ridiculed. He did however tell a number of his close friends, and in later years passed on the story to his son who by this time was working as a counter clerk in a London post office. His work at the post office was to bring a strange twist to the story, which resulted in the conversion of Green himself from a confirmed sceptic to an unqualified believer in all things supernatural.

It was just another ordinary working day when Green's son became involved in a conversation with a Scottish workman who was carrying out electrical work on the building. The conversation turned to Scotland and the name Auldearne cropped up quite by chance as a place the electrician knew well. Remembering his father's story, the counter clerk asked the electrician if by chance he knew anyone by the name of Isobel Gowdie who lived in Auldearne.

Unsure of why he was being asked, the Scotsman guardedly admitted that he did indeed know of someone of that name in the town, a woman who had lived there a long time ago. The electrician went on to describe Isobel Gowdie as a well-known witch who was involved in the witch trials of 1662. Gowdie had made long voluntary confessions without the need for being tortured. In her confessions she told of worshipping the devil, and of taking part in orgies and other sexual activities, in graphic detail.

Many of the activities involved the bewitching of local tinkers and travellers who had stopped to camp for the night in the isolated glens around the towns of Nairn and Inverness – the very place where Robin Green had been camping during that summer of 1955.

34   The Choof at Choof Cottage

On the outskirts of Grimsby once stood a row of white farmers' cottages known as 'White Row'. Towards the end of the 1700s the row had already been unoccupied for many years and had, apart from one single building, 'Choof Cottage', become derelict. A decision was made to destroy the ruins and apparently with their passing died the ghost of the 'Chimney Choof'.

It was around 1700 when a farmer's widow who lived in one of the cottages began to complain that her fire tended to blow back down the chimney. Well-meaning neighbours and relatives tried a variety of methods to prevent this, all of which were to no avail, and eventually a large thin pot, found in a nearby field, was used to replace the original one on the top of the roof. Rather than improving matters, this seemed to make things much worse and before long a local chimney sweep was called to see if dislodged bricks within the chimney stack itself were the cause of the trouble.

The innocent chimney sweep was to get more than he bargained for, if stories are to be believed, for from the moment he started to clean the chimney, a whole string of strange phenomena began to take place within the cottage.

Having managed to get his chimney sweep's brush lodged against what he took to be a loose stone in the chimney stack, the sweep had to enlist the aid of three local farmers in order to retrieve it. After heaving together for almost five minutes, the brush is said to have released itself with such suddenness that one of the young farmers fell back against the wall – cracking his head with such force that he fractured his skull and died instantly. Before the others could come to his aid, the room was said to have immediately filled with 'cauldrensful of soot' which drifted in large solid clouds around their heads, while a strange swirling light filled the air. The rickety old tables and chairs then began to rise, falling apart and crashing to the ground as they did so. At the same time, the sweep's brush dashed itself to pieces against the cottage wall.

The old lady who occupied the cottage was said to have taken a fit as a green glutinous mass of jelly suddenly emerged from the fireplace and wrapped itself round her face, her body shaking and contorting as it did so. Next followed an attack on the two remaining farmhands and the sweep himself, who by now were rigid and immobilized with fear. The men were said to have had their clothes effortlessly ripped from their bodies, whilst their genitals were 'attacked' by large globules of green jelly. These pieces of jelly had broken away from the main mass which was still pulsating around the cottage owner's face.

The screams of agony which came from the house quickly attracted other local residents, who saw soot and smoke belching from every opening in the building. Presuming that there was a fire, the local fire-drill was put into practise, and before long, buckets of water were coming thick and fast, being poured down the chimney or thrown in the door and windows.

Within a very short time it became evident that something other than a fire had taken place. Entering the cottage, the farmers found the old woman with her face completely missing, almost as if some strong acid had eaten it away. Her hair was strangely intact, though the skin on the rest of her head was eaten away to the bone. The three men were found naked (except for their leather boots and belts) and horribly mutilated, their sexual organs having been eaten away in a similar manner to the cottage woman's face. All except the sweep, who was by now a gibbering wreck, were dead. The room was covered in a greeny-black ash which gave off a terrible stench of rotten eggs. The chimney and fireplace appeared to be· in

pristine condition, and were strangely free from any of the damp ash which covered the rest of the room's contents. It was almost as if it had been newly built and had never had the smoke of fire within it.

The sweep recovered enough to tell the tale, but only lived for two or three weeks before dying of his injuries. The house remained empty for a number of months following the burial of all the victims. Eventually it was once again occupied, this time by a young farming couple and their dog. Within days the dog began whining and cowering in a corner, and strange disturbing 'choofing' noises began to emanate from the chimney. At first these 'choofs' were followed only by grunts and groans but before long a voice using language of the vilest and filthiest kind could be heard whispering down the chimney stack. It made suggestions to the young wife in sexually explicit tones, and spoke of how it would murder her husband. Determined to put a stop to 'whoever was playing the devils jest upon them', the husband sat on the ridge of the roof one night, waiting for the malicious prankster to come and speak down his chimney. Having waited two hours for his return, his young bride was said to have gone outside to look for her husband, only to find his naked body in a mangled heap at the foot of the chimney stack. He too had been sexually mutilated in the same manner as before, with only his boots and belt remaining in place.

Needless to say, following this horrendous episode, the cottage once more became empty, never to be occupied again. One by one the other cottagers left their homes in White Row, never to return. Eventually the houses became derelict, with one strange exception. 'Choof Cottage', as it had become known, had been uninhabited far longer than the other buildings in the row, yet workers who came to dismantle White Row found its interior and exterior in pristine condition, just as if it had been inhabited by some unseen occupant. The tall chimney pot, which many had claimed was the home of the 'choof ghost', was earmarked to be saved as a reminder of the cottage's strange history. As workers prised it from the structure of the main building, it apparently 'took on a life of its own', twisting itself from the workmen's grasp and falling to the ground where it shattered into tiny dustlike fragments. Despite a search by the mystified workers, not a trace of the chimney pot larger than a speck of dust could be found. It is said that in attempting to gather up some of the dust in a bag, an aged farmworker suffered an attack of sneezing so violent that he died from a heart attack – the final victim of the strange unearthly entity which had long inhabited the chimney pot.

35   The Copulating Couple

Alice was a frail old lady, about seventy-five years old, who during a bus journey from Leeds to Scarborough in 1989 struck up a conversation with a stranger who was sat next to her. The stranger was a writer of ghost stories and before long the topic of ghosts and hauntings inevitably cropped up in the conversation.

Alice said that she didn't really believe in most of the tales she had heard concerning ghosts, describing them as 'tosh', but she did reveal that despite this, she and her husband had once had a most peculiar repeated haunting. Though she was pressed by the writer to give further details, it became obvious that the whole episode had been an embarrassment to her, and out of respect for her feelings the conversation was gradually steered to other things.

Though Alice had refused to discuss her haunting, the matter must have remained on her mind during the journey, for on arrival at Scarborough she asked for the writer's name and address, promising that she would contact him by letter with full details of what had taken place.

It was almost eighteen months before the writer received the promised letter. Within the envelope was another, also addressed to him, but which had obviously at some time been torn open and resealed. Attached to the inner envelope was a short note from Alice's daughter, Helen, who lived in Halifax. Helen explained that Alice had died the month before, and while sorting through her belongings the enclosed letter had been found, opened out of curiosity and resealed.

The curious letter is reproduced here in its entirety. Only the names and addresses have been changed by request.

29 Grosvenor Road
LEEDS

August 3rd 1989

Dear Mr Gibbs,

It was nice to have your company on the coach from York last week. I'm sorry if I seemed a bit quiet regarding our 'haunting' but you see if it is of a rather embarrassing nature, and not the type of story you tell to a stranger.

It is all true I can assure you, and I have never heard anything like it and expect you won't have either, but I don't know where to start.

It was way back in the war-time when it started, the haunting that is. We lived in a very old mansion kind of building in Locksey Road, Leeds, which had been turned into flats and my husband and I occupied the whole of the top floor. Hubby was quite a bit younger than me and the only man in the building as all the other wives' husbands were at war, but he worked on the railway you see. Anyway, one night when he and I were in bed doing what married couples do we heard a moaning coming from the room next door. Hubby thought someone was watching us, jumped out of bed and put on the light next door, but the moaning stopped and he didn't find anybody about.

About a week later the same thing happened again, and just the same he didn't find anyone. Anyway we decided to set up a trap and pretend to be doing it one night. I made the noises and my husband watched through the glass panel at the top of the door, but nothing happened that time. Though we were frightened at first we rather got used to the moaning which happened every time we did it. Though we never could explain what caused it.

Anyway on one of the nights when we were doing it, we had left the door to the next room open by mistake. I looked through to where the moaning was coming from and couldn't believe my eyes because on the floor of the room was another couple doing it at the same time. I grabbed my husband's head and said, 'Look Jim in the parlour'. My husband jumped up swearing and asking what the H… they thought they were doing, but as he got up they just vanished into thin air. It was then that we knew we had ghosts.

We always left the door open after that, and always they were doing it when we were, well for a couple of times anyway, because we couldn't stand it and moved to another flat.

Who the ghosts were we don't know. No one else ever said they had seen ghosts in the building and though my hubby tried to find out the history of the building, he never came up with an explanation. The man was about thirty years old with a full beard and like a neckerchief tied round his neck, but otherwise undressed. The lady was fat and not very beautiful as I remember, and they never looked at us or seemed to know we were there, so why they joined in with us I'll never know. Anyway they never followed us to our new home, and as far as I know they were still at it in the building until it was pulled down around the 1950s.

Jim my hubby said he thought it was like a re-incarnation in reverse. You know, like us in a past life, what do you think?

Though you might find it hard to believe, I can honestly assure you that it did happen on a number of occasions. Though I have told people we had ghosts at one time, I have never ever told anybody the full facts, because of embarrassment. I suppose however at my age, I am past being shy about something which happened so long ago, and I would like the tale to live on after me, as it is so strange the likes of what no-one might ever hear of again.

Please let me know if you will use it in your book, but if you do, don't use my real name though, for my family's sake will you?

Yours faithfully

Alice Wordsworth

Sadly the writer was never able to thank Alice, but her wishes were granted, and the story now lives on after her, leaving one to wonder if her haunting was unique. What strange phenomena can motivate a copulating ghostly couple to carry out their ghostly lovemaking only when a living couple is engaged in the same act? And what, if anything, was the significance of the neckerchief?

It would seem obvious that the ghosts meant the living couple no harm, for they appeared to be unaware of their living observers. Were they, one might ask, connected in some way to Alice and Jim? Or did they perform regardless of who the living couple was? Did their sex act vary from time to time, or did it repeat the same scene, movement for movement, like some reoccurring ghostly pornographic movie? These are all questions which may never be answered – unless of course the ghostly couple are still waiting to act out their eerie coupling in some modern building which now stands on the site of the one demolished in the 1950s. Perhaps some new couple now live there, still unaware of the ill-timed spectral interruptions which may yet come to haunt their marital bed.

36   The Phantom Groper
of Borley Rectory

In 1939 the rambling Victorian mansion of Borley Rectory, Essex, was burnt to the ground. With its destruction went the legend of what is thought to have been England's most haunted house.

Many tales were told of the strange goings-on in this building. A ghost of an angry old man in a top hat would slap the face of the daughter of the rector (Revd Henry Dawson Bull) whilst she slept; poltergeists would throw items across the room; and pebbles, keys and even medals were said to have been scattered through the air for no apparent reason. Fires started mysteriously in odd places, and ghostly footsteps were heard both day and night.

Experiments with 'automatic writing' were undertaken after mysterious messages were found written upon walls and on scraps of paper. Noises of all kinds manifested themselves regularly, while bell ringing, chanting, monastic singing and medieval music were often heard at night.

Though hundreds of people were terrified by these strange events over the years 1863 to 1939, no one was ever harmed, though reputedly one of the ghosts was known to sexually molest sleepers in one particular bedroom.

The first such incident occurred in the year 1892. At that time a headless man had repeatedly been seen wandering in the bushes of the garden. Guests staying at the Bull household were given a small bedroom which until that time had been free of hauntings. The Reverend Dawson

Bull's son, Harry, who had by now taken over the house, made light of the building's reputation, and advised the unsettled guests that they were in the safest room in the house. Unfortunately it was not long before people sleeping in the room (whether male or female) made complaints that they had been visited in the night by a ghostly presence. This unseen visitor apparently made sexual advances which were intense and persistent.

In each case, the story was the same. Guests would retire to their beds only to be awakened by whispering voices. As they struggled to light a candle the flame would be mysteriously blown out and the whispering would stop. Later in the night the covers of the bed would be lifted and a ghostly hand would caress their legs and genitals. Naturally, their first reaction was to freeze in fright, but on coming to their senses the unfortunate guests would pull back the bedclothes and jump out of bed, believing they had experienced some sort of weird dream. On going back to bed the ghostly hand would once more get to work, and indignant guests were known to leave the next morning, refusing to sleep in the building another night.

Some might suspect that more worldly hands were at work and that perhaps some servant or other living person may have carried out the phantom gropings. This explanation was of course put forward at the time of the hauntings, but an experiment which included close inspection of the room for hidden panels and passages, and locking volunteers in the room all night, failed to come up with any conclusion other than that the 'phantom groper' was indeed from the ghostly realms.

No one ever saw the ghost (or disembodied hand, as the case may be), and it was found that guests sleeping anywhere else in the room (other than in the bed itself), did not suffer the unwelcome advances. Only one clue was ever given which might shed some light on the molester's identity. This came in one of the whispered messages which appeared to be spoken in the French language. The message mentioned the name Marie, together with what was thought was the French word *lait*, meaning milk. The ghost came to be known in later years as 'Marie the Milkmaid'.

Though such a living person was unknown, and this name in a foreign tongue appeared insignificant at the time, it was later discovered that in 1677 a French nun had reputedly been strangled by her lover in a building which formerly stood on the same site as Borley Rectory. One of the spirit messages which mysteriously appeared on the building's walls in the 1930s stated that her body was still buried in the rectory cellar. The nun's name? Marie Lairre.

37 Australia's Adam and Eve

Adam Trelawny was a Cornish fisherman who was transported to Australia twice, both times for sexual offences involving young men (which incidentally were never actually proved). Nevertheless, Trelawny was without doubt a homosexual, a fact which did not prevent him becoming a 'trustee', one of the well-behaved convicts in Australia who were eventually given powers of supervision over other convict workers.

Trelawny treated the men in his care with respect, but he did become emotionally involved with a particular man by the name of Edward Eves. Not surprisingly, the relationship was soon widely known about among the convicts, and before long the couple attracted the name of Adam and Eve.

Despite ribald jokes and a certain amount of good-natured banter, the relationship was tolerated amongst the convict class, who tended to keep themselves to themselves and did not pry into the backgrounds or present-day lives of their fellow workers. The authorities were either unaware of the situation or turned a blind eye. If the latter was the case, then this could account for Eves being the only member from his team of convict workers who was transferred to Parramatta (New South Wales) with Adam Trelawny, in order to work on a new road being constructed over the Blue Mountains.

Though the exact circumstances are unclear, it would appear that Trelawny became sexually involved with another convict from his new roadworks team, and before long Edward Eves found out. A number of confrontations took place and eventually Eves, in a fit of anger, was said to have smashed his lover over the head with a large rock and thrown his body over a sheer cliff.

Trelawny's disappearance caused little trouble as convicts were often escaping in order to live in the unexplored bush regions. Many thought that the trustee had simply used his position to make his escape.

It was about a week later when a gang of convicts, flattening out an area in the rocks for the new road which they were working on, spotted a naked body climbing into view. As it emerged fully into sight, the gang recognized the bloody figure as Adam Trelawny, his head smashed and mutilated on one side. Eves collapsed at the sight as Trelawny, naked and sexually aroused, walked slowly towards him and called his name. With hands stretched out like a sleepwalker, he continued to walk forward as the gang of convict workers put down their picks and watched in amazement.

Eves, still conscious, looked up from the rocky dirt track

road and screamed at Trelawny to go away. As a number of the convict road gang made moves to restrain the naked man, Eves convulsed in a massive heart attack and died, upon which Trelawny vanished immediately.

It was of course quickly realized that it was his ghost and not Trelawny himself that the whole crowd of workers had witnessed. Many said that Adam had come back for Eves – to take him with him to the next world. The convicts, including their supervisors and the army troopers on guard, at first refused to work on that section of road ever again, claiming that Trelawny would come back for them all. However, within a few days, work resumed as normal. The ridge was known for a long time as Adam and Eve's point, but the name has long since gone out of usage and all attempts to trace the exact spot have been fruitless.

The haunting seems to have been a 'one off' occurrence and no other reports of Trelawny's ghost have ever come to light. A number of wispy figures have been reported on the new highway that stretches from Sydney to Parramatta and on through the Blue Mountains of New South Wales to Bathurst. Perhaps these are simply the ghosts of the many convicts worked to death in the harsh conditions faced by Australia's first settlers.

38   The Naked Dancer
at the Royal Ball

In the mid revels, the first ominous night
Of their espousals, when the moon shone bright
With lighted tapers – the King & Queen leading
The curious measures, Lords & Ladies treading
The self same strains – The King looks back by chance
And spies a strange intruder fill the dance
Namely, a mere anatomy, quite bare
His naked limbs both without flesh and hair
(As we decipher death) who stalks about
Keeping true measure till the dance be out.
                    Heywood, 'Hierachie of the Blessed Angels'

So go the lines of an old poem describing a ghostly event which took place at Jedburgh Castle in October 1285. A number of fictitious stories have also been drawn from the event including Poe's 'The Masque of the Red Death'.

No trace of the once magnificent castle remains in modern times, though at one time it was the haunt of royalty, dukes, and earls, and was often a first choice for the celebration of royal occasions.

Alexander the Third of Scotland had been unsuccessful in obtaining an heir by his first wife and in order to put matters right, it was decided he would remarry. The chosen bride to be was Jolande (otherwise known as Joleta), daughter of the Count of Dreux. Though many rejoiced at the new marriage, others were less enthusiastic. A number of astrologers warned against the timing of the wedding, and many within Scotland were uneasy.

Despite the general unease a wedding ball was arranged in which much revelling and merriment took place. Towards the end of the evening as the king and his new bride were dancing, an almost naked male figure with an erection and dressed in dirty white rags was seen to cross the dancefloor, winding its way between the dancers. Those full of drink could do no more than giggle at the antics of the strange corpse-like figure. Its face was expressionless with a slight red tinge, and its skin appeared stretched across its hairless limbs.

A number of dancers left the floor, presuming that this was the start of some sort of show, whilst others stopped in their tracks, awaiting the reaction of the king. As he looked back towards the clamour at the other end of the room, the smile drained from his face.

'Who dare insult us with this blasphemous mockery?' cried the monarch in rage, at which a number of the courtiers made a move to restrain the figure, assisted by some of the remaining dancers on the floor. The new bride's eyes were diverted away from the figure's displayed arousal, and the unwelcome guest was quickly surrounded.

It was only at the first attempt to lay a hand upon the intruder that many realized the truth of the matter. The figure was a walking corpse, and the dirty white rags were the remains of the burial shroud hanging from his shriven body. As the figure was grabbed, it fell to the floor in a pile of dust and within seconds vanished, leaving a look of horror on the faces of all in the room.

Though no explanation could be given for the appearance of the naked ghostly corpse, or for its sexual connotations, it was generally accepted that the incident was a portent of ill-will for the marriage.

Only a few months after the wedding, Alexander the Third was dead at the age of forty-five. He was riding between Burntisland and Kinghorn when his horse reared suddenly, throwing him to the ground. Rolling along the ground, the dismounted king fell over a rocky crag and was killed instantly, although he was not found for a number of days. When he was eventually located, it is said that his dead body sported an erection like the ghost on the dancefloor, a sign, many said, that the ghostly corpse seen at the royal wedding was in fact his own.

39 Bathtime at Southerfell-side

A common argument of non-believers in ghosts is that those who claim they see them do so only because they want to, almost as if the subconscious mind transmits a picture of what one hopes to see. However, though this may be true in a number of cases where people actually set out to find a ghost, the following story shows that this hypothesis can by no means be used in all cases.

Bob Fray was a self-confessed 'ghost freak'. He collected ghost stories, visited haunted houses, and was a member of a local ghost hunters' club. He was however extremely sceptical of a number of sightings, particularly as he had personally investigated over fifty hauntings. This involved many lonely nights in haunted churches, camping out on windy hillsides, and the taking of hundreds of photographs of haunted places in the hope of capturing one of the misty spectres on film. Apart from one weird evening in a disused church, when strange tappings and groanings were captured on a tape recorder, Fray had never personally witnessed any ghostly happenings, and on a ghost club visit to Southerfell-side (Cumbria) in the 1950s, he had no reason to believe that anything would happen to change these circumstances.

The ghost club outing had been organized in an attempt to witness the 'Spectral Horsemen' which were said to appear on the 23 June each year. The vision had first been sighted in 1743 when a shepherd, Daniel Stricket, sat talking to his master John Wren of Wilton Hill (a large country house). As they looked to Southerfell-side, they were amazed to see a group of horses, followed by a man and dogs, travelling at an unbelievable speed across an area which was so steep that a horse would normally find it difficult to get across at all. As they watched, the man, horses and dogs seemed to disappear at the bottom of the fell, as though all having fallen over.

So unlikely was this vision that the master and servant decided to keep quiet as to what they had seen, for fear of ridicule from other locals. They did however climb Southerfell-side early the following morning. Despite their disbelief at what they had seen, they were reluctant to ignore the matter in case the man or any of the animals had lost their lives in the perilous dash.

As they had half-expected, no signs of hoof marks or other evidence of anyone having been at the place was to be found, and they returned home to ponder on what had occurred. Despite their better judgement the story was eventually told to local residents, and as predicted, much merriment was made of such a preposterous story.

By the following year, Stricket had left the employ of John Wren and had become servant and shepherd to Wren's neighbour, a Mr Lancaster of Blakehills House. On the 23 June (St John's Day) 1744, Stricket was going about his work, checking fences, when he caught sight of movement on the steep side of Southerfell. Moving at a quick trot, there appeared to be a whole troop of mounted soldiers on horseback, dashing across the fellside at about the same point where he had seen the strange sight before. Stricket watched for a number of minutes, until he was finally satisfied that his eyes were not playing tricks.

Rushing quickly down to Blakehills House, the breathless shepherd dragged his master from the house in order to see the curious sight. Before Stricket could point out the horsemen who still continued to ride across the scene, the bewildered gentleman spotted the phenomenon for himself. So strange was the sight that more and more people were brought out to see it.

This then, was the reason why Fray and three of his fellow ghost hunters were camping in the vicinity of Southerfell, Cumbria, on the eve of 23 June in the mid 1950s.

It would be pleasing to be able to report that Fray and

his companions spotted the Spectral Horsemen of Southerfell, but this was not the case. The evening and following morning passed by without event, and apart from a wet sleeping bag, and a miserable night, the intrepid ghost hunters had little to enter in their diaries. The visit was not totally without result however, although what was to follow did not fit the scenario that Fray and his pals had envisaged.

The time was around 10 a.m. when the trio finally began to pack up their wet belongings, ready for the journey home. A fire had been burning in order to dry out the wet sleeping bags and other items, and Fray and his friend Charlie Howard had travelled some distance from the tent in order to find firewood. As the pair followed a rough pathway through some bushes, the sound of laughter and splashing water could be heard in the distance. Walking towards the sounds, the path turned sharply at a point where the low shrubs ceased and a rough pasture lay ahead. Emerging from the wooded area the pair were confronted by the scene of a large tin bath containing a fat, naked, bearded gentleman with long curly grey hair. Splashing around with him in the tub was an equally naked, attractive young woman of about twenty-five years of age.

The wood-gatherers stood open-mouthed as the couple in the bath frolicked together, kissing and fondling each other, for what seemed like an eternity (but in reality could only have been seconds). Fray and Howard watched, not knowing whether to tiptoe away or to carry on as if nothing untoward was happening. Neither could comprehend the fact that they were seeing an old man and a young woman bathing together (and more) in a tin bath in the middle of nowhere.

While the girl in the bathtub had her back to the two friends, the gentleman seemed aware of his observers, but appeared not to be in the least concerned by their presence. Suddenly, as the young woman turned briefly, she appeared to catch sight of Fray and Howard and with a squeal, she climbed quickly out of the bathtub, spilling the bubbles onto the grass and attempting to hide behind the back of the old man, who was now laughing loudly at her antics.

Embarrassed beyond belief, the two men attempted to mumble out an apology, only to be interrupted by the old bearded man in the bath.

'Here boys,' he said, beckoning the two men towards him. Pointing towards Howard, he continued, 'You bring my robe,' and to Fray, 'and you pomatum and powder my hair ... hurry boy ... hurry.'

Taken aback by these strange orders, Fray and Howard looked at each other, open-mouthed, only to return their gaze to the tub and its contents. By now both the girl and the man had almost vanished completely.

In disbelief the bedraggled pair, still clinging to their firewood, watched as the old man quickly became a shadowy figure, barely visible against the background of the hillside. His hands continued to beckon, and his mouth appeared to be still uttering words, though by now they could not be heard. Fray was dumbstruck. Though aware of a strange chill feeling and the hair on the back of his neck standing up 'like porcupine quills', he felt strangely pleased to have seen his first ghost. Howard on the other hand (as he was later to freely admit) wet himself with fear, and had to be led back to their waiting and bewildered friend in a state of shock.

Strangely, the sighting of the ghostly pair in the bathtub led to the demise of the ghost club. Having been confronted first hand by the real thing would seem to have taken the interest out of the subject for the three. It would be interesting to know who the bearded old man and his bathmate were, and why they appeared in that isolated spot, far from the site of any known building. Could it be that the man was connected with the spectral horsemen, perhaps a commander who had once taken such a bath in a tent on the site? It is known that armies in ancient times had young women followers who would travel around the country with the soldiers, in much the same way that 'groupies' follow pop stars today. But surely such an army commander (if that is what he was) would not colour and powder his hair as this particular gentleman obviously did (if we are to remember his directions to his two boy attendants). Fray and Howard had obviously, by some strange mistake in the mechanism of existence, unwittingly crossed the barriers of time to take the place of those boy attendants.

The ghostly bathtub couple have never been reported again, and it would seem that this is yet another instance of a single unexplained occurrence of a momentary haunting. That the haunting did occur is undisputed, for it was witnessed by two separate people. Two people who were so shocked by their encounter with the ghostly realm that they were not prepared to follow the story further, leaving yet another enigmatic mystery and a multitude of unanswered questions.

40   The Pregnant Ghost

Within the Church of Saints Mary & Cuthbert, Chester-le-Street (County Durham) are a series of fourteen ancient effigies portraying the ancestors of Lord Lumley, a sixteenth century nobleman. In 1680/81 the village of Lumley (which took the family name), became the centre-point of a local scandal which rocked the whole of northern Britain. In addition, the mysterious circumstances of the revelation of the body of a murder victim (by ghostly means), ended in a controversial trial where the evidence of the ghost was accepted as valid by the prosecuting judge. In the event, two local men were sentenced to death and executed on the day of the trial.

It is said that a well-to-do widower named Walker, who lived in the village, had decided to take on a housekeeper. Despite a number of applicants locally, Walker decided to bring in a young relative (some say his niece, some his granddaughter) named Anne Walker, to fill the position. Despite the great age difference between the two, it was not long before rumours began to circulate that Walker and his relative were sharing a bed, and within just a few weeks she is said to have become pregnant.

In order to cover the matter up, Walker apparently arranged for the young girl to stay with an aunt named Dame Cave in nearby Chester-le-Street. Disbelieving neighbours were told that she had not liked domestic life, and had returned home.

Despite the local scandal, matters died down, though Walker feared it was only a matter of time before someone in the village discovered the girl's whereabouts. Such an event would blacken his respected name and damage his reputation as a man of good character. With a friend, Mark Sharp, Walker hatched a plan to take the girl from the area altogether. The pair convinced Dame Cave that they had now found a place of safety in Lancashire for Anne Walker to live with her expected baby. Walker was to support the girl and her offspring, whilst a relative of Sharp would look after her safety and welfare. Consequently the young girl packed her belongings and left the area with Walker and his cohort.

Within a fortnight, both Walker and Sharp had returned, telling Dame Cave that the girl was now comfortably set up for life. The villagers by now had other things to occupy their minds and to Walker's relief, life went back to normal in the area.

Walker once more settled down to a comfortable existence, confident that his reputation within the community had been re-established. Unfortunately for him, matters were already going drastically wrong. Within two days of his return to the village, an event took place which was to seal the fate of Walker and his friend Sharp, forever.

A mill owner named Grahame the Fuller was working in the early hours of the morning, finishing a special job for a local merchant. As he began to shut up the mill and blow out the candles in the upper floor, he heard a noise down below. Descending the stairs with a candle burning in his hand, he became aware of the figure of a young woman standing in the centre of the floor. As the only light came from the candle he was carrying, he was unable to see her face.

'Who is it?' he asked, wondering why such a young girl should come to his mill after midnight.

'It is I,' said the girl, 'Anne Walker.'

In disbelief, the miller moved towards the figure. He could now see it was indeed Anne Walker, though her face was not that of a living being. Her skin was a deathly pallor and her dishevelled hair was covered in blood from five large wounds upon her head.

Assuring the miller that she meant him no harm, the ghost began to reveal the whole story, saying that Walker had made her pregnant, and had then hatched a plot to kill her and bury her body upon the moor.

'When I was sent away with Mark Sharp, he slew me on the moor with a collier's pick, and threw my body into an old coal pit,' she said.

In disbelief at what was happening, Grahame the Fuller sought more details, asking how she might prove that what she said had taken place was true. Without further ado she undid the laces on the front of her dress and revealed her breasts.

'See,' she said, 'these are the swollen breasts of a mother to be, and this,' she said, widening the front of her gown further, 'is the swollen belly of the same.'

'Cover yourself, for I am a married man and do not wish to see your body,' cried Grahame modestly. 'If what you say is true, where shall I find your body?'

The girl proceeded to give directions as to where her body might be found. In great detail he was directed to a rocky bank where the pick had been hidden, and then to where the murderer's blood-covered shoes and stockings were.

'You must tell the magistrate, so that justice can be done,' she said, and with this the image vanished, leaving the perplexed miller to shakily make his way home in the dark.

Some months passed and Grahame, not wanting to accuse such a stronghold of the community on such strange evidence, took to leaving his mill before nightfall, obviously in an attempt to ward off any further sightings of the ghost. However, on a particular occasion whilst working in the mill some months later, time had got the better of him. Realizing the coming darkness, Grahame attempted to rush home, but in the early dusk the bloodied pregnant ghost once more appeared and repeated her story.

The following morning (with much embarrassment), the miller visited the local magistrate to tell his strange tale. To his surprise the Justice of the Peace believed his story and immediately ordered a search in the area described. Within a short time, the body, the pick axe and

the bloody shoes and stockings had been found just as the ghost of Anne Walker had predicted.

Mr Walker and Mark Sharp were subsequently arrested and in August 1681, Judge Davenport heard the strange details of the circumstances leading up to the discovery of the body.

The whole of northern England was alive with talk of the trial, particularly the damning evidence of Sharp's own footwear which had been found at the scene covered in blood. Walker protested his innocence, declaring that the judge could not possibly convict such a well-respected man as himself on the evidence of a ghost, and stating that any judge who did so would become a laughing stock.

Walker's conceit was to cut no ice with the judge, for he was indeed found guilty. Still protesting his innocence and threatening an appeal to parliament, Walker said that he would not wish to be in the judge's seat when all this came to an end.

Unfortunately for Walker, his end was to come sooner than he was to realize. On pronouncing the two men guilty, the judge ordered their execution that very evening.

Never in the history of Durham jail had such a speedy execution been ordered, nor was one ever to occur so quickly again. Neither, as far as it can be established, has any man, either before or since, been brought to justice on the evidence of a pregnant ghost. This was a strange situation indeed, for we are presented with a case where the ghost of the murdered woman was able to lead the authorities to the finding of her body and to the murder weapon used to carry out the crime. The guilty verdict proclaimed by the judge against both parties ensured that Anne Walker had received the justice she sought. She had successfully brought her murderers to justice in August 1861, despite the fact that she herself was already dead by this time, and had been since the murder took place on the Durham moors in 1860. Indeed, this must be one of the most strange murder trials in the history of the British legal system.

41 Murder and Rape at Winnats Pass

For almost a decade the unearthly sounds of murder and rape were to be heard on summer nights in Winnats Pass, Derbyshire. Travellers would report hearing the sounds of struggles and fighting, followed by screams. Next would come the sound of a woman's protesting voice, followed by the sexual grunts and moans of people obviously in the act of sexual intercourse. No one at the time was aware of the story behind the disturbing noises, but following the discovery of a male and a female skeleton by miners digging out an old shaft, the sounds of rape and murder were heard less and less, and gradually information was put together which began to explain the strange events of the previous ten years.

The story begins in the mid 1700s when Winnats Pass was the haunt of itinerant miners who would go there to work, pick up their pay, and move on. Though the area was a peaceful one, law and order was virtually absent, and locals worried little about the motives of those who came and went in the district. Among these 'comers and goers' were a number of young couples, usually under age, who would visit the area in order to get married without any questions being asked. It was one summer's evening when such a couple turned up at a local inn near the pass, asking for directions to Castleton. Having refreshed themselves and conversed with a number of miners, the couple set off on their way. Sadly they were not to know that among the miners they had spoken to were a number of ruthless criminals who, fortified with drink and full of thoughts of money, followed them out and took a short cut to Winnats Pass to wait in ambush.

Having dragged the couple into a miners' hut, they were quickly relieved of their savings, and were ordered to strip to their underclothing in order to prove that they had no other hidden money or valuables upon their person. After being ogled lustfully by all the miners, the young girl was pleased to be allowed to dress and the miners went outside, leaving the couple shaken but thankful that they had come to no harm. Their troubles were not yet over however, as they found themselves locked inside the shed. Despite all attempts to free themselves from their wooden prison, the couple realized that there was little chance of escape until they could attract the sound of other travellers passing by and they sat down to wait.

Returning to the inn, the miners hurriedly began to spend their newfound wealth. Discussions now took place on what should be done next. Opinion was split two ways; half the miners suggesting that they should take the money and run, the other half wanting to kill the couple so that their robbing activities would not be discovered.

Eventually, full of dutch courage from their bout of heavy drinking, and filled with lustful thoughts of the young undressed girl they had seen earlier, the miners returned to the hut intent on killing the young couple. The lad was easily overpowered and despite the protests of his young bride-to-be, he was brutally slain with a pickaxe. Next came a terrible sexual assault on the girl by all the miners. An attack so vicious that she was said to have died almost immediately.

The haunting which was prompted by these actions came almost immediately. It is said that as the miners returned after dark to dispose of the bodies, the sounds of their own attack on the couple could be heard emanating from the hut. Despite their fear, the effects of the heavy drinking session had not worn off, and at last, one of the group opened the hut door to find nothing but the two dead bodies and their belongings.

Everything, including the couple's clothes, were divided amongst the group, and the naked bodies were thrown into a deep disused mine. Rumours quickly spread in the closeknit community, and though it was suspected that something sinister had taken place, ranks were closed and the matter was forgotten after one of the miners involved hung himself in despair. It is said that the other conspirators all met violent ends within a short time of the tragedy, and it was only with the discovery of the two skeletons ten years later that the story was pieced together from snippets of information given by friends and relatives of the murdering miners.

Though the repeated haunting sounds of rape and murder virtually ceased with the grisly discovery of the young couple's skeletons, there are still occasional reports in modern times of strange panting sounds and groaning coming from Winnats Pass. Sometimes a scream or a muffled cry is heard, as are the sounds of shouting male voices. Occasionally too, a ghostly couple have been seen scrambling arm in arm up a sheer rock face or climbing diagonally across a buttress. Many say that these are the spirits of the murdered young couple, after all these years still endeavouring to escape from the deadly clutches of the drunken miners who so brutally took their lives in the lawless days of the eighteenth century.

42 The Screams of the Homosexual King

In Barklaye Castle died a King
And yet his agonised cries do ring
His ghostly screams and dying breath
Still linger to proclaim his death.

On earth in water he was born
He died through fire and a hunting horn
A score of years he lived so fair
In death his screams still fill the air.

Anon

Berkeley Castle, Gloucester, is the scene of one of the most gruesome events in the history of British royalty, for within its walls, King Edward II (1307–1327) was most brutally and sexually murdered. It is said that occasionally the taunting voices of his capturers can be heard, muttering obscene taunts, before the terrified cries of the dead king give way to agonizing screams. If high emotion (as many people believe) is a precursor for the presence of ghosts, then it is little wonder that such an event as occurred at Berkeley Castle on 20 January 1327 has impressed itself on the very fabric of time. The castle itself is an impressive, stately building, but in times past it had a somewhat sinister reputation, under the ownership of one of the previous lords of Berkeley. It is said that the castle well had become stagnant and had ceased to be used as a water supply. Instead, it became a general waste disposal pit, where household waste, dead animals and other general rubbish was disposed of. Tales are told of people being thrown alive into the well at the pleasure of the lord, who ruled his nearby subjects with an iron glove. Some say that a tiny well-house was once built above the well in order to stop the stench from the rotting bodies in the stagnant waters below. Those who were lucky enough not to be thrown in were reminded of their narrow escape by being imprisoned in the damp and windowless well-house above.

The gory story behind the obscene, taunting voices and the bloodcurdling screams of the dying king begins in this well-house, where King Edward II was said to have been imprisoned after his capture under the orders of Queen Isabelle, whose lover Roger Mortimer had seized the power of the throne. Mortimer's daughter married Lord Berkeley, and it was through this connection that the king found himself imprisoned at the castle.

Edward II was a known homosexual, and suffered continuous taunting and perhaps sexual torture from his jailers during the period of his imprisonment. Despite the mental torture he had to endure, and with little food and appalling conditions, Edward was a resilient and strong character. Even after a period of some months, and to the dismay of his captors, Edward showed no signs of dying from his deprivations. Eventually word came from Queen Isabelle that his captors should find means of speeding his demise. Orders were given to leave no marks on his body or other evidence which might lead to later accusations of torture or murder.

A sickening but effective method was drawn up which the captors believed would be an apt and fitting end for the homosexual king. Edward had by now been moved to a chamber in the castle where pains were taken to ensure he was well fed. He was also given medical attention for his wounds and sores to convince observers after his death that the king had been well treated in captivity.

On the evening of 20 January 1327 he was dragged from his chamber to a bare stone-walled room in the castle. Here the terrified king was stripped of all his clothing and spreadeagled face down upon the floor, his hands and legs tied to prevent any movement. Accounts vary as to what took place prior to his horrendous execution, but it is widely believed that a number of objects may have been inserted between his buttocks – possibly to accompany the taunts of his captors regarding his homosexuality, but certainly in preparation for the final insertion of a small wide-necked powder horn which was to allow a quick and certain means of execution for the captive.

As the king lay manacled to the ground, with a number of his captors sitting upon him to prevent further movement, a red hot poker was carried into the room and unceremoniously inserted through the horn into the bowels of the deposed monarch.

Though short-lived, it is said that the king's tortured cries were of such volume that they reverberated through every room in the castle, and could be heard by workers in the fields ten miles away. It is the king's blood-chilling agonized death cries (so intense that their effect appears to have endured over hundreds of years) that are still to be heard, and which still have the ability to strike fear into all who are unlucky enough to be receptive to this disturbing event from the past.

43   The Ghostly Pick-Up

Nicholas Prior was a Birmingham solicitor of little note, other than the fact that he had a rich client who resided in London who always insisted upon Prior taking charge of his legal affairs. It was the practise of the unnamed rich client to invite his solicitor to London perhaps a week, or even two, before he was to carry out any particular legal work, so that he could 'study the papers'.

Prior quite enjoyed his paid 'legal jaunts' as, unknown to his client, most of the time whilst in London was engaged in 'doing the town' on expenses. Prior was a single man and on his return to Birmingham, would treat his colleagues in glorious detail to tales of his various sexual exploits whilst in 'the big smoke' as he called it.

It was in June 1930 when, having returned from one of these trips, the solicitor appeared to be far from his normal self. Friends begged him for his usual titbits of sexual titillation, but Prior remained relatively silent, saying only that he had had a good time.

Eventually, a few weeks later, and under the influence of a certain amount of whisky, Prior's friend (a doctor named Jenkins) succeeded in drawing out of the reluctant solicitor tales of an experience which had shaken him so much that he had resolved never to return to London again.

Having dined at an expensive West End restaurant, and having drunk a large number of whiskies, Prior had taken a cab to one of the areas of the city known for its 'better quality good time girls', where he wandered around, surveying the scene.

Having been propositioned a number of times, he

decided to move on to another area, and looked for a passing cab. As he waited, he was approached by a young respectable-looking girl, who seemed to come from nowhere. She literally seemed to form out of the fog, whereupon she asked him for a light. Prior confesses to not knowing whether the pretty young girl of about eighteen years of age was a prostitute or not, for she seemed to be dressed more like a member of the aristocracy than a common prostitute. She was of medium build, with long silky hair. She wore a ring on her wedding finger, and a broad-rimmed hat. Her long flowing dress was covered by a dark, heavy coat and a kind of cape, of the kind that nurses often wear. Prior distinctively remembered her piercing blue eyes and kind smile.

The couple evidently talked for a while without bringing up the matter of whether or not the young woman had approached him with prostitution in mind. Prior persuaded her to 'have a drink', and eventually a strangely painted cab with a blue and white chequered door was hailed which took them to a nearby hotel bar. Throughout the journey the young woman said nothing. Prior assumed she was slightly embarrassed by being picked up in such a manner, but he himself found it hard to make conversation in the confines of the multi-coloured interior of the cab.

As the cab drove off into the distance, and before the couple could step into the hotel bar, the mysterious woman engaged Prior in such a passionate kiss that he was quite taken aback. When he eventually did respond, the woman became more and more passionate, begging him to book a room in the hotel immediately, saying that he should come back and give her the room number so that she could follow him up.

It was at this point that Prior established that she was indeed a prostitute. However, she insisted that this was her night off, and such a handsome gentleman as himself would not be charged a penny for what was to follow. Prior now began to suspect (because of her accent) that this was the well-to-do daughter of some local lord or dignitary. He also suspected, despite what she said, that she was not in fact a prostitute, but was acting out the part as a fantasy for her own sexual satisfaction. In popular parlance, she was 'slumming it for kicks'.

However, Prior said nothing, and could not believe that such a passionate, beautiful young stranger was about to share his bed. He soon booked a room, and returned to the hotel door where he passed the room number onto the waiting woman.

Going straight to the first floor bedroom, Prior waited. Within minutes, the young woman joined him and during the hours that followed, the young solicitor was treated to such lovemaking skills as he had never known. The insatiable appetite of his companion left him exhausted, but despite his protests he was pestered and cajoled into performing again and again, until he literally fell asleep through sheer exhaustion.

Prior next remembered being awoken once more by the exploring hands of his young companion, at which he stated that he just could not go on. He avoided the young girl's clawing fingernails and quickly attempted to get dressed whilst still laid across the bed. Sensing his resolve, his companion's mood changed quickly and violently, and to his horror her beautiful young face contorted into that of a raging lunatic. Spitting and cursing him in the vilest language, the young woman stood above him, violently scratching at her own body with her long fingernails, and spitting upon him as he lay in terror beneath her. Her eyes then turned bloodshot and red, and her toenails appeared to grow, twisting and turning as they did so. By now Prior was hypnotized by the terrible transformation he was witnessing. Her skin had become old and wrinkled, and her hair appeared to glow with a strange yellow light. Dark red weals now rose up on her body where her own fingernails had drawn blood. Paralysed with fear, Prior could only watch as the young woman completed her transformation into an ugly old hag.

As suddenly as the transformation had begun, it ceased. Prior, still crouched in fear beneath the woman on the bed, watched in amazement as the beautiful young woman returned, her skin seeming to stretch and resume its youthful vigour. The weals on her body mysteriously healed and disappeared, and her toenails now reverted to their normal state.

As she gazed at him, her eyes expressed amusement at Prior's predicament. He opened his mouth to speak, but was prevented from doing so by the gentle pressure of her right forefinger on his lips. She herself did not speak, but proceeded to fade into a misty shape before his very eyes. Though he could feel the pressure of her finger, he could now barely see her as she slowly disintegrated before him. Finally, only a faint outline of her face could be seen, as her lips uttered her last words.

'A ghost,' she said with amusement, 'just a ghost.'

With this she vanished completely, leaving Prior to hurriedly dress, his mind desperately trying to comprehend the experience.

Still in a state of stunned confusion, Prior left the hotel and hailed a passing cab. It was the same strangely painted taxi which had brought the couple to the hotel. The driver greeted him cheerfully, and Prior responded by asking if the man knew the young woman who had accompanied him there earlier.

'There must be some mistake, sir,' said the cab driver. 'You were alone when I picked you up.'

Assuring the cab driver that it must be he who was mistaken, Prior went on to describe his companion.

'Some around here might laugh sir,' the driver said seriously, 'but that's the second time this week that someone has said the same thing to me. Only three days ago, I picked up a young gentleman at the same place as you, and brought him back again. He must have had a drop though sir. Said she'd turned into an old witch whilst he was in bed with her. Some odd people round here if you ask me ... '

The young solicitor tipped the cab driver, but decided to walk to allow himself time to gather his thoughts and pull himself together.

During the next few days Prior investigated the matter, asking other cab drivers in the area if they had seen anyone matching the description of the young woman with the wide-brimmed hat. None had. Strange to say, none had even seen a cab with a blue and white chequered door and a multi-coloured interior. On further investigation, Prior himself could find no indications of any such cab ever existing on the streets of London and became convinced that it and the driver were also from the ghostly realms. To his dying day, Prior repeated his belief that if he had taken the return journey in the strangely coloured cab that June night in 1930, he would never have lived to tell the tale.

44   The Butchered Bride

Though the ghost of Susan Young is referred to as 'the butchered bride', she never actually married. Neither was she truly butchered, though a savage sexual attack left her bleeding and near death. Susan died as a result of a cruel joke at the hands of a group of three youths – who had once enjoyed her 'liberal company' but had later become disenchanted with her promiscuous ways.

Tourist leaflets refer to the ghost as the 'white lady', telling that it regularly haunts a village inn in the county of Buckinghamshire. Toned down descriptions of the haunting tell how visitors to the inn have seen a lady in white drifting from room to room, or have found her lying upon their beds as they retired at night.

Other versions tell a more gruesome story of a bleeding corpse in a tattered wedding dress, lying twisted and almost naked upon a bed in the inn. One such tale has been related by Jean Daniels who stayed at the village inn many years ago. During the evening as she retired to her bed, Jean became aware of a feeling of intense cold in the room. Thinking that it was just a particularly cold night, she slipped on a long T-shirt. Strangely though, twice during the evening she awoke in a sweat from a disturbed dream. Though she could not remember the contents of the dream, she was aware of either herself or someone else being sexually attacked by a group of men. On the second occasion she removed the T-shirt and went back to sleep. Again she was disturbed by the strange half-dream and unable to settle, decided to get up and visit the toilet.

On her return, she was terrified to see the body of a young near naked girl, on her bed and covered in blood.

She immediately recognized that the girl was dressed in a bloodstained wedding dress which was ripped completely down the front and held to her body only by the fabric of the sleeves. Petrified with fear and not knowing whether to run or to go to the bedside, she decided on the latter. However, as she reached the bed the figure simply vanished into thin air. Distraught as she was, Jean did not feel that she could reveal what she had seen to the landlord, for fear of being thought somewhat odd, as there was no sign of bloodstains or anything else untoward in the room. Getting dressed, she remained awake until morning, when she paid her bill and left.

Mrs Daniels' tale is certainly not unique, and gives credence to a story which is told of a young Buckinghamshire barmaid named Susan. Susan preferred men to call her Sukie. Though she was only sixteen, she was already an experienced and attractive young woman. Her mature body and youthful playfulness was greatly popular with the males in the area, and her flirting was encouraged by the landlord, who realized that it brought increased trade to the inn. Unfortunately, Sukie was well aware of her charms, and delighted in playing up to one male, then another, causing a certain amount of jealousy amongst her admirers. Stories do vary somewhat as to the exact circumstances which led to her downfall, but it would seem that three local farmhands had already asked her to marry them. On each occasion she had said yes, only to tell the disappointed young man later that she had not really meant what she had said. One of these youths had already bought her a wedding dress, and Sukie kept it in her room at the inn, refusing to give it back.

A regular guest at the inn was a rich young merchant, and rumours were that each time he visited the village, Sukie shared his bed. Eventually she was asked by the rich young man to marry him and she accepted. This time Sukie meant what she said, and a date was fixed, much to the anger of the local youths, particularly the one who had bought her the wedding dress which she now planned to wear.

A plan was drawn up by the local lads to get their

revenge on the barmaid. Though it started out as a cruel joke, circumstances were to lead to a more serious conclusion. A note was left at the inn, supposedly from her future husband, saying that she should meet him in nearby caves the following evening. Sukie was told to wear her wedding dress.

The evening came, and Sukie gathered her long dress around her waist and paddled her way through the undergrowth towards a light she could see in the cave where she had arranged to meet her lover. Sukie was now full of romantic visions of being swept off her feet and carried by horseback to some waiting priest who would marry the couple by moonlight. To her disappointment and horror, she found not her future husband waiting for her in the cave but the three drunken youths she had previously promised to marry, obviously now intent on gang rape.

Though she fought bravely, the treacherous youths ripped her wedding dress from top to bottom, and one after another repeatedly had their way with her, until they suddenly realized that her body was now lying limp and almost lifeless on the cave floor. Panic set in as they saw what they had done – the young girl was now bloody and unconscious. Shocked and sobered by their own actions, the three hastily decided to carry her back to the village and put her in her room, in the hope that the rich merchant would take the blame for what had taken place.

Records do not relate how her body was found, though it is certain that Sukie was returned to her bed, and later died from her injuries. How long her almost naked and blood-soaked body lay upon the bed in its torn wedding dress is not known, but the story has endured over the years as a horrifying reminder of a young girl's tragic betrayal and death. It is also a story which re-emerges from time to time when her ghostly image reappears unexpectedly, to haunt unsuspecting travellers staying in her room at the welcoming Buckinghamshire country inn.

45 The Suckling Witch

Knaresborough, in Yorkshire, was once well-known for its witches. In 1621, Edward Fairfax accused six witches from Knaresborough forest of bewitching his children. They were brought to trial at York, but thanks to the proverbial commonsense of the northern judges, were found innocent of all charges. It is said that after the judgement was pronounced, the Fairfax family were mobbed by the assembled crowd, and narrowly escaped with their lives.

Undoubtedly the most well-known of the Knaresborough witches was Old Mother Shipton, who it is said lived in a cave near the river, and who successfully prophesied a number of modern inventions including the telephone, railway and motor car. The 'Dropping Well', close to Mother Shipton's former home, is now a tourist attraction where visitors leave objects such as hats, gloves and teddy bears to be magically turned to stone through the effects of the constantly dripping, mineralized waters within the cave.

A ghost which haunted a wood between nearby Ferrensby and Flaxby was sighted regularly in the days before the A1 was converted into the modern motorway that it is today. However, between 1948 and 1955 there was only one appearance, and by all accounts this was the last time that the 'the suckling witch' (as it had become known) was ever seen.

It was believed that 'the suckling witch', when alive, was a member of one of the many witches covens which apparently existed in this area. The apparition has never been positively connected with any particular living person, though it is known that in the 1800s she was known as 'Mother Kitty'. Whether this was her actual name or a reference to the cats which were connected with this particular haunting, is not certain.

It used to be believed that when 'Mother Kitty' appeared, local cows would have problems with milking, and it is said that once a local farmer took it into his own hands to slaughter every cat he could find in the neighbourhood, in order to 'put Kitty to rest', a task in which he proved unsuccessful.

The reason for the slaughter of the cats soon becomes clear. On each occasion that she was sighted, the witch was to be seen suckling a different cat with milk from her own breast. Though the haunting occurred in exactly the same manner and in exactly the same part of the wood on each occasion, the cat was said to be different in each case. It was widely believed that cats which had sucked at her breast were responsible for 'cow fevers', a term that covered any manner of bovine ailment in the days before veterinary care was widespread.

On eight separate occasions in 1898, 'Mother Kitty' was seen in the wood. Each time, she was described as sitting in the hollow of the same deformed tree, her dirty blackened garments open to the waist, and her wrinkled hands gently stroking a cat which was sucking milk from her exposed breast.

It appears that up until the 1930s, reports of the witch's appearance in the wood were quite commonplace. After the Second World War sightings were intermittent, and her image appeared to be fading quickly at each appearance. The last person to spot 'Mother Kitty' (who by now attracted the more modern name of 'the suckling witch') was a young biologist on a field trip in 1955. Having wandered off alone, he was surprised to see what he described as 'obviously a ghost, sitting with a real cat upon its lap'. The young man had not heard of the ghostly figure, and was surprised to have his story totally believed by the landlord of a nearby public house when he returned to meet his colleagues at lunchtime.

The young biologist had entered the wood in search of insect life which he was collecting for research purposes,

when suddenly he became aware of something sitting in the hollow of a tree ahead of him. He described his experience as follows:

I was immediately aware that I was looking at a ghost, though I was strangely not frightened by the sight. She appeared to be about eighty years of age and extremely wrinkled with a large pointed nose. She looked exactly like you might imagine a fairy story witch would, though she wore neither a pointed hat, or any other form of headgear. I have always wanted to see a ghost, and tried communicating with her, shouting hello and asking her name. This brought no response and she neither looked at me, nor spoke a word. In truth I don't think she was even aware of my presence.

I took particular notice of her clothing which seemed to be a single piece of tartan-like cloth in various shades of brown, which was tied around her waist with a piece of torn cloth in the form of a belt. Her eyes looked down, rather kindly I thought, at a cat in her arms which was laid on its back and close to her chest. Though I could not see any details from the distance I was at, I was aware that the top part of her clothing hung open, fully exposing both her bare bosoms which were not wrinkled (as I would have expected), but more like those of a young woman. Though I was told later that the ghost was known to allow cats to suck at her breasts, I cannot honestly say I was aware at the time that that is what was happening, though it is certainly probable, judging from the position of the cat at her chest and the fact that her bosoms were bared.

I hesitatingly moved forward slowly, and saw that the foggy-looking character of the ghost was in total contrast to the cat which was solid and very real-looking, having the same grey colour as the old woman's hair. When I was within six feet or so of the ghost, it simply disappeared, letting the cat fall naturally to the ground, twisting round and landing comfortably on all fours on the grass. The whole experience couldn't have lasted more than two or three minutes.

I was more shaken by the sudden disappearance of the ghost, than in being confronted by it in the first place. The cat seemed unconcerned, and walked slowly towards me. I stroked its back (really I suppose to check that it was a real cat and not another phantom, but it was real enough I can assure you). It then wandered off into the bushes as though nothing unusual had happened.

Since that strange appearance, the witch was seen no more. Whether she had finally faded into oblivion, or whether the noise of modern traffic from the nearby busy roads had some profound effect on the haunting, is not known. Locals no longer seem to be able to identify the tree (if it still exists), or indeed the wood in which the haunting once regularly occurred. Some even deny any knowledge that the ghost ever existed, though at nearby Scriven, at least two old residents still insist that the milk-yield records from all the farms in the area show a marked increase from the very day 'the suckling witch' disappeared forever from the district.

Bibliography and Further Reading

Alexander, Marc, *Enchanted Britain* (A. Barker Ltd, London 1981)

Bradbury, Will, (ed.), *Into the Unknown* (Readers Digest Assn, 1988)

——, *Phantom Encounters* (Time Life Books, 1988)

Briggs, Katherine M., *Nine Lives (Cats in Folklore)* (Routledge/Kegan Paul, 1980)

Carnforth Jnr, Charles, *A Strange Case of Death* (B.H. Printers (U.S.A.), 1959)

Crowe, Mrs, *Night Side of Nature* (Unknown, c. 1830)

Elworthy, Frederick Thomas, *The Evil Eye* (Julian Press, New York, 1986)

Gettings, Fred, *Visions of the Occult* (Rider, 1987)

——, *Folklore Myths and Legends – Britain* (Readers Digest Assn, 1973)

Grant, George, *Tales from the Marshes* (Privately published 1901)

Green, A.M., *Northern Folk Tales (Part 1)* (Publisher unknown, 1879)

Green, Celia, and McCreery, Chas, *Apparitions* (Hamish Hamilton, 1975)

Halifax, Viscount, *Lord Halifax's Ghost Book* (Bellew Pub. Co. Ltd, 1989)

Herbert, W.B., *Railway Ghosts and Phantoms* (David & Charles, 1989)

Ingram, John H., *Haunted Homes and Family Legenas* (W.H. Allen & Co. (no date))

——, *Strange Stories, Amazing Facts* (Readers Digest Assn, 1975)

Jones, Gareth, *Visitations of Death* (Self-published essay, 1923)

King, Francis, *Cult and Occult* (Orbis Publishing, 1985)

Lofthouse, Jessica, *North Country Folklore* (Robert Hale, 1976)

McEwan, Graham J., *Haunted Churches of England* (Robert Hale, 1989)

174

Mackenzie, Andrew, *Dracula Country* (A. Barker Ltd, London 1977)

O'Donnel, Elliot, *Ghost Hunter* (Foulsham, Slough, 1991)

Peach, Emily, *Things That Go Bump in the Night* (Aquarian Press, 1991)

Robinson, P.H., and Hesp, P., *Ghosts (Beverley & East Riding)* (Hutton Press, Beverley, 1987)

Robson, Alan, *Grisly Trails and Ghostly Tales* (Virgin Books, London, 1992)

Timbs, John, *Abbeys, Castles and Ancient Halls* (Warne & Co, London, 1870)

——, *Curiosities of England* (Warne & Co, London, 1870)

Turner, Jim, *Broken Axles and Blanco* (Privately published, 1957)

Underwood, Peter, *This Haunted Isle* (Harrap Ltd, 1984)

Welton, Guy, *Students' Guide to Ghosts* (Publisher/date unknown)

Westwood, Jennifer, *Albion* (Book Club Associates, 1986)

Whitaker, Terence, *Ghosts of Old England* (Robert Hale, 1987)